# Capturing Personality in Woodcarving

### E. J. Tangerman

Sterling Publishing Co., Inc.  New York

## Other books by E. J. Tangerman

Carving Faces and Figures in Wood
Carving Flora and Fables in Wood
Carving Religious Motifs in Wood
Carving Wooden Animals

**Library of Congress Cataloging in Publication Data**

Tangerman, E. J. (Elmer John), 1907-
   Capturing personality in woodcarving.

   Includes index.
   1. Wood-carving—Technique. 2. Wood-carved figurines
I. Title.
NK9704.T24       731.4'62       81-50979
ISBN 0-8069-7530-X (pbk.)       AACR2

Copyright © 1981 by Sterling Publishing Co., Inc.
Two Park Avenue, New York, N.Y. 10016
Distributed in Australia by Oak Tree Press Co., Ltd.
P.O.Box J34, Brickfield Hill, Sydney 2000, N.S.W.
Distributed in the United Kingdom by Blandford Press
Link House, West Street, Poole, Dorset BH15 1LL, England
Distributed in Canada by Oak Tree Press Ltd.
% Canadian Manda Group, 215 Lakeshore Boulevard East
Toronto, Ontario M5A 3W9
*Manufactured in the United States of America*

# Contents

*Fig. 1. Textured Indian head, Vancouver. It is heroic in size and over-painted, but the texturing is dramatic and powerful.*

# Carving Personality – and Why

CALL SOMEONE AN ARTIST and the layman will ask, "Oil or watercolor?" He forgets that there were nine Muses, and the so-called fine arts include sculpture, poetry, prose, and dance, among others. Use the word "portrait" and your listener will ask, "Of whom?" Even Webster's supports this view with the definition, "a pictorial representation of a person." The use of that word for "a picture of an object" is now called obsolete. There's a similar problem with the word "image."

What we are seeking to capture is a *personality*, whether it be of a person, some other animal, or of an inanimate object. What this book deals with is individual likenesses, representations of specific animals, flora and inanimate objects so that they are distinct and recognizable.

We begin with a chapter or two on depicting the general shape of things other than people, then progress to attaining likenesses of such diverse subjects as a house, a barn, other models, a profession, a hobby, a dog or two, and ultimately portraits of people. Included are such ideas as how to copy a statue in miniature and how to make masks of animals and people.

In short, I've tried to explain how to carve a likeness of just about anything. This is a frequent challenge to any woodcarver, whether he be amateur or professional, neophyte or skilled. Many of the examples here described were commissions, because many customers want likenesses, if they can get them, particularly of something near and dear to them.

I have tried to arrange the chapters in order of difficulty, the easiest first and so on. I have shown some projects in more detail than others, depending upon the number of rough spots I encountered. Some pieces are shown in step-by-step photos; where I felt they would be useful I have provided patterns. I have avoided specialized language and specialized tools, and tried to select examples that cover a wide range of subjects. Included, as usual, is basic information on tools, woods, and sharpening, plus added notes chapter by chapter. Additionally, there is information on changing the size of patterns and on finishing carvings, either in color or in natural-wood finish. Enjoy!

E. J. Tangerman

# CHAPTER I
# What Wood to Use

## Local availability, subject and finish are factors

YOUR CHOICE OF WOOD USUALLY DEPENDS UPON TWO FACTORS: what is available and what you plan to make. Old-time whittlers used whatever they had: willow for whistles, fruit woods for small figures, ash or hickory for tool handles, and so on. Nowadays, most whittlers begin with soft woods such as white pine, basswood and jelutong (a recent import from Indonesia) because they are fairly soft and readily available—the first two at the local lumberyard. None has a very prominent grain, so there is usually a need for staining or tinting to lend distinction.

The woodcarver, on the other hand, tends to use harder woods like cherry and black walnut, even oak and maple, or imports like mahogany, which will support more detail, take a better finish, and have some grain to give them variety. All of these are much harder to cut than pine or basswood, but that is not particularly important when you use chisels.

There is also considerable variety in the woods used, because of their local availability as trees. Thus, red alder and myrtle are carved on the West Coast, ironwood and osage orange (both very hard) in the Southwest, buckeye and basswood in the Northeast, walnut in the Central States, tupelo (cottonwood) and cypress among others in the South. Eastern mountaineers use holly and fruit and nut woods like pecan. South of the border, Mexican carvers work an endless variety of woods because Mexico has more varieties of wood than any other country, some 2,800.

Basically, the easiest way to determine what wood to use initially is to try it with the tools you intend to use. Many whittlers simply buy wood at the local yard, or even send away for blanks to round up and shape, because that's easier and less "messy" and requires no extra tools.

In this book, I have tried to show, piece by piece, what wood I or other carvers used, but this is merely a suggestion. Of American woods, the best is black walnut, which is medium-hard, does not splinter easily, and takes a fine finish. But it does tend to warp and check if exposed to weather, and it is quite dark unless bleached. I prefer teak, particularly for outdoor use. It is lighter in color, immune to insects, rot and similar decay, doesn't warp or check to any extent, and can be finished simply with oil. When oiled, it is a warm brown; when left to weather, it turns grey. Mahogany is also a fine common wood, but it comes from many sources and varies widely as a result. I have six samples from the Philippines, all called mahogany but varying all over the lot in hardness, density and color. Among the best of the mahoganies are those from Central America.

Among familiar and softer woods are poplar, which bruises easily and tends to grip tools, so is hard to cut; cedar, which is easy to cut but tends to crumble and has a distinctive color; willow, which tends to split; cypress, which does not wear well. Butternut, red alder and myrtle are easy to carve. Redwood (sequoia) is durable but tends to have alternating hard and soft layers that can cause trouble. Most yards have soft maple, which isn't particularly good to carve; on the other hand, hard maple is.

Among the imports, rosewood usually can be carved, but it is hard. Like ebony and lignum vitae, it is very expensive. Most of the African woods, like beef, bubinga, zebra, thuya and the like, tend to split and are a nuisance to carve. This is true of purpleheart, greenheart (from Brazil), and vermilion as well, but these three woods have distinctive colors and therefore make fine pendants, for example. There are dozens of other woods, some with extremely elaborate "figure" (that may interfere with your carving) like harewood and satinwood, for example. Then there is pink ivory, the most expensive wood of all, a delicate pink-white to red in color. If you can afford it—and find it—it is interesting to work. But, in the end, the choice must return to what you can get and the effect you want to create.

*Fig. 2. Bovine group for a Nativity scene was whittled from white pine and antiqued with sal-ammoniac stain. The bull is 3 in (8 cm) long. Better quality figures can be carved from pecan or holly and not tinted.*

## CHAPTER II
# Tools Should Be Simple

### The whittler needs only one; the carver uses a variety

THE BASIC TOOL OF THE AMERICAN WHITTLER is the pocketknife. The word "whittling" means to work with one tool to pare away wood, so it could be applied to a totem pole made with a shingling hatchet or to a figure carved with an adz, or even an axe handle shaped with a spokeshave. But the common understanding is that whittling is done with a knife, to produce a one-piece object usually small enough to be held in the hand. Most whittlers saw out the blank, and sand it when finished, so they have actually used at least three tools, but they only count the knife. The old-time whittlers started with only a branch and a knife—and ended with them.

That's really all you need to whittle, a branch and a knife. It helps to have an idea and to develop some skill, which this book is intended to help provide. If your idea is to produce likenesses, however, you'll want more than a knife before you're through, because a knife, although it is the most versatile tool, creates problems in carving concave surfaces and shaping details.

If you are getting a new knife, select one with two, or at most three, carbon-steel blades that are relatively short and pointed. I carry two knives. One is a jackknife with pen, spear, and B-clip blades, the other is a penknife with pen and B-clip (see Fig. 3). At home I use fixed-blade knives with larger handles; they're less tiring on the hand and safer. One of these is pen-shaped, another B-clip, and the third a "hook" or pull blade with a slender tip and concave edge. Two of the three have chuck handles with interchange-able blades. All are carbon-steel (stainless doesn't hold an edge as well). And don't be taken in by handles with finger shapes or other projections; they limit versatility.

The basic cutting stroke in whittling is similar to that used in paring a potato: the thumb braced against the surface, the knife caught in the four other fingers, and the force applied by closing the hand. This provides maximum control of the cut, but can be hard on that projecting thumb if you're not careful. Some beginning whittlers use finger stalls of leather or rubber to protect the thumb (stationery stores sell the latter for sorting papers).

There are many other strokes or methods of cutting suited to particular purposes; you'll learn them as you go, as I did, but here are some pointers:

A pushing cut with the arm, as you'd make when cutting a point on a stick, is safe but not very effective, except for roughing, because it is hard to control; a draw cut, in which you hold the knife like a stiletto and draw it toward you, is good for outlining, but tends to run with the grain. This tendency can be reduced by holding the knife the opposite way, with index finger extended along the blade heel and the knife sloped in the direction of the cut, rather than vertical. I find that I often use either thumb or a finger on the back of the blade to apply greater force to a cut, and use a thumb or forefinger of the opposite hand on the heel to combine force and control on precise cuts.

To whittle successfully, you must learn about grain. It is easy to cut with the grain, but beware of splitting, and over-cutting. Cutting across the grain is far more difficult and slower, and cutting diagonally can cause the knife to follow the grain. Grooving and modelling can readily cause splitting; it is vital to cut across grain first, making what is known as a "stop cut." The knife must be kept sharp, very sharp for soft wood. It helps to oil it occasionally to inhibit rusting caused by pocket sweat; also, avoid cutting paper or fingernails and peeling wire with it, and always be conscious that the blade is hinged and that it can easily close on your finger.

The woodcarver has a much broader range of tools. In fact, he can and does use any tool he likes or has available, the object being to get the waste wood out of the way, not to do the entire job with one tool. Thus, primitive carvers use axes, adzes, saws, even fire in rough-shaping, and rasps, files, sandpaper (even if it is just sharkskin) in finish-shaping. The American penchant for mechanizing has introduced power equipment, of course, including band, chain and circular saws, power sanders, pneumatic and electric hammers, routers, even rotary power tools.

Some carvers depend almost entirely upon a particular power tool and select designs to suit its limited capacity. Thus, a carver of totem poles or wooden Indians relies mainly upon the chain saw; the carver of primarily commercial gadgetry, such as miniaturized shoes, relies on a rotary tool; and the decoy carver mainly uses rasps. These carvers also make extensive use of specialized all-position vises, hoods, safety glasses and respirators, because they are primarily concerned with production, and power tools generate dust and danger.

The typical chisel is somewhat specialized in function, so it is necessary to have several to suit various cuts. This is particularly true if you make likenesses. The most familiar shape is similar to that of a carpenter's flat chisel, except that it is thinner and is sharpened from both sides so it can

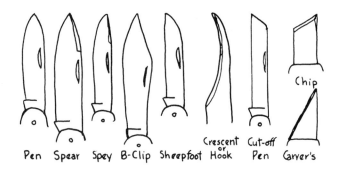

*Fig. 3. Knife blades.*

cut without digging in. It is called a *firmer*, and is available in widths from about $\frac{1}{16}$ in (1.6 mm) to about 2½ in (6.4 cm) wide.

Then there are the *gouges*, available in a similar size range, but varying in sweep or angle of curvature, and sharpened on the outer side only. They are commonly classified under the so-called London system, ranging from #3 to #11 or #12, the lowest numbers being almost flat, while the highest numbers are U-shaped in cross-section. The gouges are commonly used for roughing and general shaping, as well as for grooving, because they do not catch at the edges as a firmer tends to do.

The firmer has also been modified to have a diagonal edge, and is then called a *skew*. It may have a rounded cutting edge, in which case it is called a *bullnose* and can be used instead of a flat gouge to cut a concave surface or to smooth a flat one.

There are also some specialized chisels, like the *parting* or *V-tool*, which cuts a V-shaped groove; the *macaroni*, which cuts a square-bottomed groove; and the *fluteroni*, which cuts a similar groove, but with rounded corners. The latter two are rare among amateurs and have limited usefulness, but the V-tool is practically an essential. Although difficult to sharpen, it is one of the most versatile of chisels.

Wider gouges, which would be heavy and clumsy with straight sides, are available with a narrowed shank, and are called *spades* or *fishtails*. All types can also be obtained with bent shanks for undercutting or shaping tight spots. The angle of the bend may be long or short (*see* Fig. 4) and even a semicircle, in which case the gouge is called a *spoon*. There are also gouges with a reverse curve, called *backbent* tools.

Many of these specialized shapes are like specialized knives; they're suited only for the repetitive making of some arbitrary shape, like grapes or leaf edges on cuckoo clocks, and I almost never use one—another chisel or the knife usually will meet my limited requirements. It takes more cuts but saves the time of locating and stropping the special tool.

The beginner in woodcarving has a great many choices of tool size and shape, many recommended by particular teachers or experts, and many put into kits, complete with case, by the arbitrary decision of some manufacturer. Handles can be round, octagonal (so they don't roll), or plastic (ugh!). Also, the standard shapes may be purchased as short tools with palm handles, like an engraver's burin. These again are handy for miniature work, but almost useless if you intend to use a mallet and do carvings of any size. We also now have available Japanese-style tools, with very short blades and long handles; American carvers will find them too slow and fragile for most work.

Your selection of chisels will depend almost entirely upon what you are likely to be making. A good starter set will include four or five tools, a flat gouge (#3) ⅜ to ⅝ in (9.6-16 mm) wide, a ⅜-in (9.6-mm) #7 or #9, a ¼- or ⅜-in (6.3- or 9.6-mm) V-tool, a ¹⁄₃₂- or ¹⁄₁₆-in (1- or 1.6-mm) #11 tool, called a *veiner* because of its primary use, and possibly a ½-in (12.7-mm) firmer (#1). No fancy shapes or skew chisels. Much of my work involves elaborate shapes and detail, so I find I make greatest use of tools in the ⅛- and ¼-in (3.2- and 6.3-mm) range, both gouges and firmers, smaller than the "starter" group. I almost never use a skew chisel—the knife works better for me—nor do I use bent tools. I find spade tools, even as narrow as ¼ in (6.3 mm), handy. I also make little use of riffler files and never use a rasp because I dislike the resulting torn surface.

To a considerable degree, these are matters of personal preference. I have no studio worthy of the name, merely a carpenter's bench with a machinist's 4-in (10-cm) and big carpenter's vises, a power router, a saber saw and a ¼-in (6.3-mm) power drill with sanding disk. Neighbors have band saws they're happy to lend me. Much of my carving is done with the piece held in a vise or lying loose against a stopboard on a bench, or even on my lap in the Oriental fashion, because I like to sit down next to the fireplace or on the back terrace, where again I have a heavy table. You may want a more elaborate setup, with a tool rack, or a carving stand with lazy-Susan top, or whatever. Such accessories are up to you. (The bench should be higher than normal if you are going to be standing up.) You will also need, of course, some familiar carpenter's tools like planes, scratch awl, compasses,

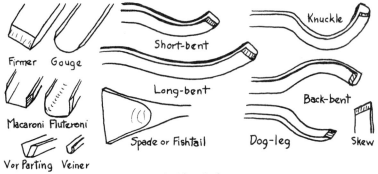

*Fig. 4. Chisel shapes.*

scroll saw, clamps, and the like. If you plan to do 3D statuettes, a carving stand and carver's screws (*see* Appendix III) are comfortable answers.

Carving differs from whittling in that, except for palm or small tools, you need both hands for the tools, so the work must be set solidly to stay on its own a great deal of the time. On softer woods and larger designs, the tool handle is gripped with one hand while the other holds the blade to guide and restrain the tool against what may be an over-enthusiastic arm push. I rarely do close carving with the tool alone; I tend to use a light mallet of the potato-masher variety because I can control the cut more precisely that way. Some carvers hit the butt of the tool with the palm of one hand, but that leads to hand damage. There are now mallets of various weights and shapes available, as well as various materials.

In relief carving, the first operation is to lower the background around the subject. This is done in a series of steps. The first is to outline the subject with the V-tool or veiner to define the shape and break the surface fibers to reduce fraying. Then a small firmer or gouge is driven in vertically along the V-cut to deepen the outline. This is called *setting-in*, and is best done in two or three steps if the wood is inclined to split, the waste wood outside being removed with a flat gouge between steps. This is called *bosting*.

When the desired depth is reached—often as little as ⅛ in (3.2 mm) on small panels—the background is leveled with the flat gouge and firmer in turn; this is called *grounding-out*. Large areas of background can be power-routed, a considerable saving in time and easier from the standpoint of uni-form depth. Carpenters also use a hand router for such work. If the subject is simple, you may want to texture the background, which will make it appear darker, because a rough surface reduces light reflection. On most woods, such texturing can be done with stamps having simple designs; one of the simplest is created by filing a cross on the flattened end of a spike. Such texturing also reduces the need for an absolutely plane surface, as does "antiquing" (finishing with dark stain), which I prefer.

As might be expected, the problem in learning to use gouges and the V-tool is grain. Any tool that cuts a groove diagonally across grain tends to drag on one side because that side is entering new fibers, and on some woods this can result in splitting or fraying. The primary answer is practice and very sharp tools that are kept that way. You will also learn that a gouge that is an arc (low numbers) can be twisted slightly back and forth as you push, so some slicing action occurs. This is a useful trick for hard spots and knots or "sticky" woods like ash. Another help at times is to move the top of the tool handle from side to side, although this can create a jumpy or wavery cut. Using a mallet usually avoids such difficulties.

If your piece is too big to hold in a vise, and not big enough to stay still under tool pushers or mallet blows, you can hold it in a variety of ways. The simplest is just a stopboard, a slat nailed across the bench against which the work is pushed. Another is to clamp the work to the bench or table, or to drive a nail or two through waste wood into the table. To avoid marring a table top, you can put a stop slat on a piece of plywood larger than the work and clamp that to the table, or put a nail or screw from the bottom of the plywood into base or back of the work. For a readily portable stopboard, add a second slat on top to create a rectangular pocket on the backboard, and fasten another slat securely to the near edge of the bottom to rest against the table edge.

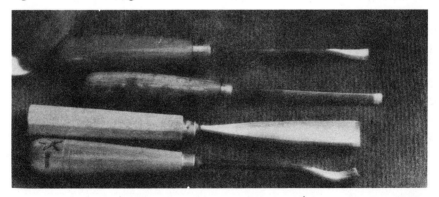

*Fig. 5. One-inch (2.5-cm) deep gouge, ½-in (12.7-mm) flat gouge, ⅜- and ½-in (9.5- and 12.7-mm) bent gouges; all are excellent for hollowing.*

**13**

## CHAPTER III

# First: Likeness of the "Breed" or Type

### Brasstown carvings must meet an accepted pattern

THE FIRST STEP IN ACHIEVING A LIKENESS is to attain a general similarity. You must be able to carve a pig before you attempt to carve a particular one. For centuries primitive carvers have carved the familiar objects around them, and the more gifted or trained among them have gone on to carve the personality of particular individuals—portraits (if I can be forgiven the application of a word usually restricted to representations of people). This is a fundamental urge all carvers have: to carve a recognizable likeness.

This is not easy. It involves careful study of the individual to see how that individual differs from the norm, particularly in the face and head. It is relatively easy to duplicate bulging muscles, a flat or bald head, a crippled limb, but harder to emphasize the smaller, and more important, variations. If you fail, you have a caricature at best, but more likely a cartoon.

The layman is most critical of an attempt to carve a human, because he is best schooled in the differences between individual people. But it is just as important, if you are carving an animate or inanimate subject, to be able to see how that individual subject varies from what the observer expects, and to stress those variations enough so that you have a likeness. Regrettably, a great many carvings of such subjects are inaccurate, and hence lose what I might term a sympathetic treatment. You can put a trunk on a post and call it an elephant, or add a forked tongue to a grub and call it a snake, and perhaps get away with it. But the keen observer sees the difference and rates your carving accordingly.

To try further to convey the idea of a true likeness, I have selected a series of examples of standardized figures from Brasstown, North Carolina (Figs. 6–19). They are likenesses of the breed, not of the individual, but the likenesses are required to meet a critical standard. They must not vary. They are what they are, and no mistake. The simple fact that they have been sold successfully for over half a century is proof positive that they are basically correct, individual, and recognizable—and, more than that, alive.

Brasstown, North Carolina, is far west in the Smokies, a tiny town not on many maps, two hours by car from Chattanooga. It has been, for more than 50 years, the home of the John C. Campbell Folk School and the site of what is, as far as I am aware, the only cottage woodcarving industry in the United States. The school provides blanks and instruction to local mountaineers, who carve simple figures which the school finishes and markets. Most of the carvers are women, and they carve familiar animals in fruitwoods and some Nativity figures in holly, which are finish-sanded and given a couple of coats of Deft® at the school before being sent to various gift shops around the country. Local carvers use the knife basically, but supplement it with the rasp, sandpaper and a few chisels, some of them homemade from ice picks or whatever. And most of the carvers are specialists, some of them capable of developing new designs, while some make the same designs they learned many years ago from someone at the school.

Most of the designs are relatively simple, except for the Nativity figures, and such figures as sleeping kittens, which I have always found to be rather difficult. They actually are a short course in carving animals. In any case, I have assembled some of the more common designs here, some of the pieces being taken from the collection of Val Eve, who worked at the school for some years. Most are self-explanatory and not particularly complex once the blank is sawed. The usual woods are buckeye, white pine, basswood, holly, and various fruitwoods, all locally available, and occasionally walnut.

One additional note: The skills of people who supply the school vary widely, and many are quite specialized. Jack Hall, who also teaches, is a versatile carver noted for his horses and Nativity figures; Ruth Hawkins is noted for her angels and cherubs; Hope Brown for her cats. All designs were developed by the individual carvers.

*Fig. 6. Present-day Brasstown carvings include cardinal, leaping squirrel, baby camel, black bear and land turtle. Each was made by a different carver and has the standard sanded and polished finish, with two coats of Deft®.*

**15**

Figs. 8–9. This maple wren, life-size, is mounted on a natural knee.

Fig. 7 (above). Prancing horse, in cherry, is one of the designs for which Jack Hall has become famous. He works from sawn blanks, with knife and rasp and tiny chisels made from ice picks for details.

Polished surface

Fig. 10 (left). Ruth Hawkins is famous for her angels and cherubs. This carving is in ¼-in (6.3-mm) holly and is about 2 in (5 cm) tall. Hands and braid are fully detailed, as is the face.

Fig. 11. Caricatures are uncommon; this gosling was made by a student.

Fig. 12. Goose girl, by Hope Brown, is a special design carved in holly by her alone.

Fig. 13. The lean and rangy hound is a popular subject. Two of these show gaunt ribs; the third is sleeker and less detailed, made by a less-skilled carver.

*Figs. 14–16. Domestic animals are familiar subjects. Here are cows, pigs and goats, all relatively simple and undetailed.*

*Fig. 17 (above). Two of Hope Brown's many cat designs, in buckeye, each about 4 in (10 cm) long.*

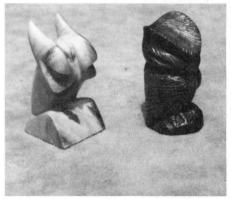

*Figs. 18–19. Owls are favorites among collectors. The single owl is by Dexter Dockery, in buckeye and mounted on driftwood. The other two (above, left to right), in buckeye and cherry, are from nearby Cherokee, North Carolina, carved by Cherokee Indians. They are much more stylized, the cherry one elaborately textured and finished with too much gloss varnish, but the shapes are good.*

## CHAPTER IV
# Skaters Are Unit Mobiles

CARVED THREE-DIMENSIONAL PIECES need not necessarily stand on bases. Indeed, a base can occasionally detract from the piece, particularly if the base is strongly figured, too ornate, or seems incongruous, as it sometimes does beneath a fish or a flying bird. Instead, the figure can be suspended from thin wire or nylon monofilament, even though it is "heavy" in the mind's eye. Suspension gives the carving life in the sense that it will move, and also will show all sides better than with a lazy-Susan base or unaided.

I have, at one time or another, made a variety of figures to be suspended from a light fixture, shelf, bracket, in a window, or even on a Christmas tree. Some were simply silhouettes, but most were three-dimensional, and some showed surprising life, i.e., a bird with spread wings, or a snake carved in a spiral, or a trout taking the fly.

This particular group (Figs. 20 to 31) was a commission from a lady who is a skate dancer, who has four sons who play hockey, and who wanted something decidedly different for Christmas-tree decorations. These include two Dutch boys (one upset), a girl, a dancer, models of old-fashioned Dutch skates, crossed miniature hockey sticks and several beavers (alluding to the name of the boys' club). The people were made in basswood, jelutong, or Alaska red cedar and tinted with oils; one pair of skates is of mahogany, the other of cherry; all were finished with flat varnish. The hockey sticks can be whittled easily (and carefully) from cigar-box mahogany and the pucks cut from dowels. Skate runners—and in the case of modern skates, the entire skates—are cut from thin metal and shaped by filing. I used aluminum for most, but brass shim stock for two tiny pairs, just for variety.

Fig. 20. Frisian boys in historic costumes, each of tinted one-piece cedar. Skates had strapped-on wood bodies and inserted blades with slightly differing sled fronts.

*Figs. 21–22. Peggy Fleming skating backward, a likeness made from a Sunday supplement snapshot, is about 6 in (15 cm) tall and one piece except for skates, which are thin aluminum with saw-toothed tips. Wood is jelutong, tinted with oils.*

*Fig. 23 (right). Frisian girl wears vintage costume and Wichers de Salis skates, an old type with strap-on wood body and inserted metal blades. Figure is tinted basswood, about 5½ in (14 cm) tall.*

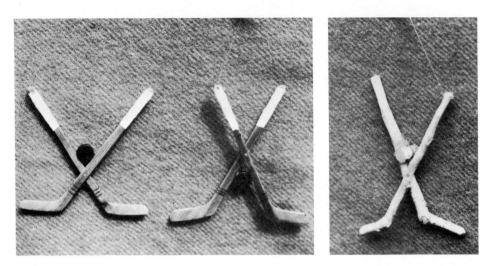

Figs. 24–25. *Crossed hockey sticks with puck (left) are 4 in (10 cm) long; puck is
⅝-in (16-mm) dowel. Sticks are varnished and trimmed, with tape-wound handles.
At right, for contrast, are crossed "shinney" sticks whittled from twigs, with miniature
soup can for puck—the poor-boy version of hockey.*

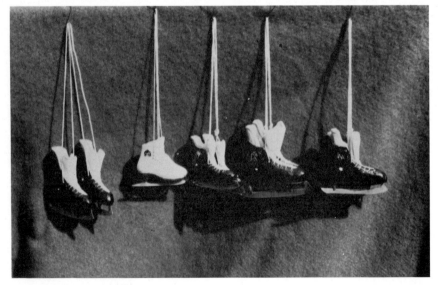

Fig. 26. *Four pairs of graduated-size miniature hockey skates and a pair of ladies'
dancing skates, the longest about 1¾ in (4 cm), whittled from basswood and tinted.
Drilled holes in upper shoe cuffs are laced with thread-braided laces, which provide
a method of hanging as well.*

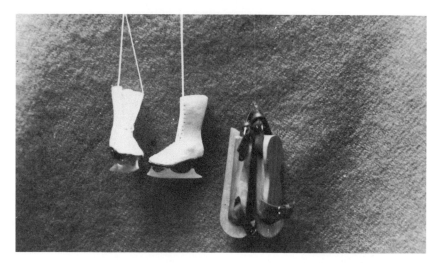

*Fig. 27. Ladies' skates circa 1910 came high above the ankle. Beside them is a pair of all-wood skates, the commonest homemade farm variety both here and abroad for centuries.*

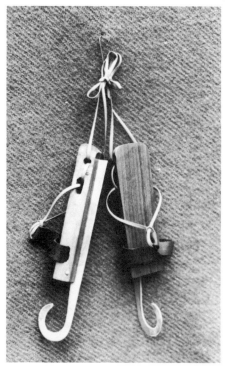

*Fig. 28 (above). Three pairs of miniature skates about 2 in (6 cm) long include two of bone, showing earliest single lacing and later multiple-type. At center are antique adjustable-sledrunner beginners' skates with wood body and metal runners.*

*Fig. 29. The Hollandse (Dutch) skates at left were among the fancier varieties, with ankle thong and double toe-stirrup. These are cherry.*

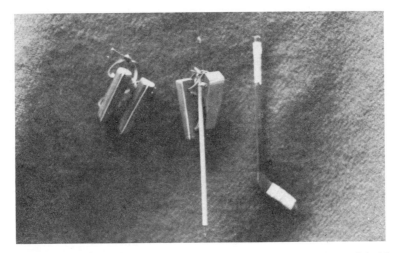

Fig. 30. First skates after the bone ones were simply blocks of wood held on with thongs. The wearer pushed himself along the ice with a pronged pole (center). Legend has it that an error led to the first skates with a metal plate on the edge, which reduced wear and friction and made skating as we know it possible.

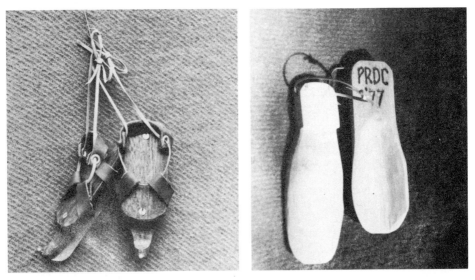

Figs. 31–32. A rather elaborate skate used well into this century is the Frisian (left), with wood body and metal runner. Straps formed a sort of sandal when laced on. These are mahogany, with gilt beads. Shoe horns at right in the shape of shoe soles are of maple, with incised lettering. About 6 in (15 cm) long, they are mementos for a skaters' committee.

Apparently, older skates had rather simple fastenings, usually just straps over heel and toe held together with thongs tied between. There were variations, however. The Dutch style had a loop incorporated in the forward strap through which the thong was passed, and no heel strap; instead the thong passed through the rear slot, up around the heel, then back through a rear circular hole and forward to be tied at the instep. Also, the Frisian skate and Wichers de Salis skate had a two-part heel strap joined at each side by eyelets through which the thong was threaded. And the Frisian skate did not have a continuous front strap, but rather a through-strap with sewn end loops, so the thong could be tightened at the toe as well. The Frisian skate also sported a small gold ball at the front.

Through-slots on the model skates were produced by drilling three small-diameter—about $\frac{1}{16}$-in (1.6-mm)—holes side by side, then joining them by cutting out the filaments with a long, thin blade. (They can also be dummy slots with the strap ends glued in.) I cut the straps from thin leather and used goatskin lacing for thongs. On the tiny skates of the figures, I carved the straps, but not the thongs; all can be painted on more easily.

Obviously, compact figures such as these will not be much affected by zephyrs, but projecting elements like raised legs and the boy's flying scarf will increase the tendency to rotate. In any case, they hang free and move—which is the object. I have also included several pairs of whittled old boots and loafers (Figs. 32 to 36), intended for pendants. The beat-up boot, in various forms, is a favorite project for many beginning whittlers, because slight variations do not matter. It is, in a sense, a caricature of a shoe.

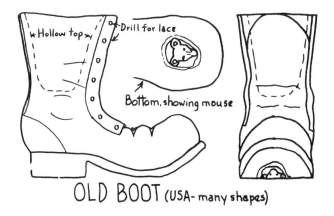

OLD BOOT (USA- many shapes)

*Figs. 34–36. Here are whittled boots in various sizes, two with mice peering through holes in the soles. The small ones and the loafers at top and above were made into pendants.*

# CHAPTER V
# Pose Figures in Action

## Low relief solves problem of unsupported elements

ACTION POSES GIVE LIFE AND MOVEMENT to figures and carry them out of the stiff and mediocre "portrait" pose. Your sports pages are full of photographs that can be converted into such carvings, and they can readily be enlarged or reduced to suit your needs by the method of squares (*see* Appendix II). The resulting carving will be understandable even to the most casual observer. You can start with general reproductions like these, then progress to likenesses.

However, carving a sports figure in the round is complicated by the gear involved. A racquet, golf club, bat, or other item of sports gear is difficult to carve, because it is usually both fragile (in the carving) and carved across grain. What's more, the figure's extended arms and legs can pose similar problems with grain.

One easy way around these headaches is to carve the figure in low relief, thus letting the background support the fragile elements. These examples (Figs. 38 and 39) happen to be skaters. The two panels were copied same size. The wood was Oregon white pine, 1 × 9½ × 11¾ in (2.5 × 24 × 29 cm), with the grain running crosswise for convenience in carving extended limbs. (There is no rule that says grain must run vertically; it's just the custom. Also, the horizontal grain gives flow to the composition.) The six other figures (Figs. 40–45) are silhouettes in teak, each enlarged from old lithographs or from my own designs.

Each panel figure was, in effect, placed across a shallow bowl, roughly delineated and textured with gouge cuts about ½ in (12.7 mm) deep at the center. Bowl diameter is about 7 in (17.5 cm), selected so an extended element will cross and break the circle to provide some feeling of stability and motion out of the "spotlight." When carving was completed, the plaque was spray-varnished (matte), then "antiqued" with a darker stain (teak), which was immediately wiped off the high spots. The result is a carving that seems to be much deeper than it is and an accentuation of the highlights. Such a composition need not be limited to single figures; I have sketched two other skating pairs to show what I mean (Fig. 37). Either pair would be difficult to carve in the round, and extremely fragile as well, but they are relatively easy in relief.

Fig. 37.

PAIR SKATING
(Irina Rodnina & Aleksandr
Zaitsev, USSR, 1976 champions)

(Tai Babilonia &
Randy Gardner, U.S.
1976)

PAIR SKATING

The silhouette panels can actually be whittled, but then are easier and faster when carved with a combination of tools. The sawed silhouette gives the form, of course, but there is a considerable amount of wood to be removed in modelling the figure. Preliminary roughing can be done with ⅛- and ¼-in (3.2- and 6.3-mm) firmers and ¼- and ⅜-in (6.3- and 9.6-mm) low-sweep gouges, and shaping of edges is much faster with a ½-in (12.7 mm) firmer than with the knife.

Pleating on dresses, lines in hair and similar details go faster with a veiner or V-tool or fluter. The scallop pattern around the jacket of one young lady can be outlined and set in with a ¼-in (6.3-mm) medium-sweep gouge. A ⅛-in (3.2-mm) flat gouge and a ⅜-in (9.6-mm) medium-sweep gouge are helpful on details and molding of skirt lines. Thus I found myself using a pocketknife for facial details, a heavier knife for heavier cutting, a hook knife for corners, and about ten chisels for specialized shapes and major wood removal.

Originally, I carved the buttons on the boys' jackets, but I replaced the simple shape with copper tacks (first filing the heads round!) to give a spot of color. I used round-headed brass brads on the top-hatted gentleman's coat for the same reason. It's not orthodox, but it looks good, at least in my opinion.

Teak 1 in (2.5 cm) thick was selected for these figures because they were to be placed in a somewhat humid location and possibly exposed to weather. They ranged from 6 to 12 in (15 to 30 cm) tall, and were finished with a Danish oil. The Dutch figures were adapted from my own earlier designs, the American ones taken from a lithograph of the period and enlarged.

*Figs. 38–39. American speed skater in the 1976 Olympics (left) is 1 × 9½ × 11¾-in (2.5 × 24 × 30-cm) Oregon white pine, framed in a 7-in (18-cm) circle. Textured background is antiqued with a darker stain, while snow at edge of course is stylized and interrupted to express the planar surface of the ice. Grain runs crosswise to suggest motion. At right is Peggy Fleming performing a back spiral—again, across grain. Checks were prevented from spreading by a vertically grained ¾-in (19.5-mm) backboard that also sets the plaque out from the wall. The 7-in (18-cm) circle on 1 × 9½ × 11¾-in (2.5 × 24 × 30-cm) Oregon pine suggests a spotlight.*

**29**

*Fig. 40 (left). This Frisian girl of about 1880 wears Wichers de Salis skates (runners inset aluminum). She is about 8 in (20 cm) high and has a fluted skirt. Skate details are whittled.*

*Fig. 41 (above). Frisian boy of the same period, wearing Doorlooper (rink) skates of aluminum, has suffered a mishap. He is about 6 in (15 cm) tall and is hung from the upper hand. His jacket buttons are copper nails.*

*Fig. 42. Frisian boy (at left), companion to the girl, wears Outerkirk skates of aluminum and has copper tacks for buttons. He is 8 in (20 cm) tall. All three of these carvings have been enlarged from mobile elements in the preceding chapter.*

Figs. 43–44. Girl and boy are enlarged from a skating print of about 1860 set in Central Park, New York. She is 9 in (23 cm) tall, he 10 in (25 cm). His cap tassel is whittled separately and inserted for strength. Skates are aluminum.

Fig. 45 (right). Formal skating couple are also enlarged from an old skating print. Man's coat buttons are round-headed brass nails; lady's muff is appliquéd to get desired grain. Overall height of the pair is 12 in (30 cm).

# CHAPTER VI
# Carving a Model – an Introduction

WHEN I WAS A CHILD IN INDIANA, each summer I awaited the visit of the touring "Swiss Village," an animated town with people about 6 in (15 cm) tall and housed in a wagon. My father, a machinist, made and repaired models. A Christmas present, too expensive for me, was a model steam engine that really worked. I saw models in store windows, museums, and shops, and I made my own—some animated, some static, ranging from the very simple to the complex—with subjects such as a castle and a lighthouse, a Boy Scout camp layout, houses, barns, and cars. Even in business, later, I made models: miniature men to illustrate a three-dimensional chart, power plant equipment for magazine-cover photographs, etc. Later, I exhibited miniatures of hand tools and machine tools much better made by others. They were always fascinating, both to me and to most other people.

I suppose every boy at heart is a model builder, as is every grown craftsman. Almost every whittler is a model builder in a sense, for what is an in-the-round figure, a decoy, a windmill? All are models. And a model builder must be a whittler as well, because the knife is the most versatile of tools and wood the most versatile of materials, be it only for patterns for metals or plastics. Of course, any model store these days has a variety of kits with plastic and metal parts for model ships, planes, boats, autos— whatever will appeal to the person without the skill or the desire to make his own from scratch. Somebody, however, whittled the originals.

The secret of good model making is accuracy and attention to detail. You *must* get a likeness, even though it is mechanical or geometric. Two other points that I must mention about models are that they tax your ingenuity and that you will be able to use up not only many otherwise too-small wood scraps, but also some of those odd bits of metal and other materials that you've been saving for so long. I find myself using little bits of ivory, brass, bronze, aluminum; for instance, I used a found wedding ring for a crown, a tiny silver cross in a steeple, an odd-shaped bit of metal for the central figure in a fountain, and so on. Models provide an excuse to paw through all sorts of out-of-the-way stores, and they provide a great opportunity to show off your ingenuity. And it's something to talk about—modestly, of course—when the model is displayed.

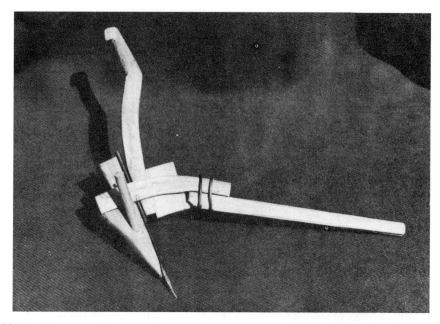

Figs. 46–47. This set of farm tools of a bygone age was whittled from oak by a farmer in Trujillo, Spain. It includes a complicated plow, rake, maul and one-piece spade. Scale is about 1:6.

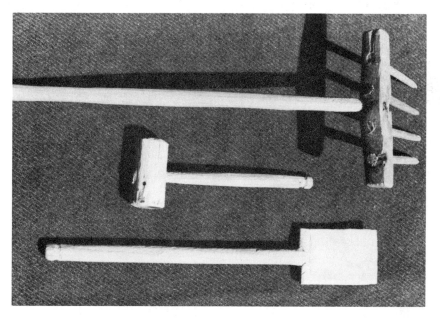

*Figs. 48–52. Before World War II, I photographed this model of the 1746 shop of "Thos. Shaw, Cabinet Maker & Turner." It was complete with working lathe (belt-driven), stain-mixing and painting area, tools, fireplace and products (Fig. 52).*

Fig. 49.

Fig. 50.

*Fig. 51.*

*Fig. 52.*

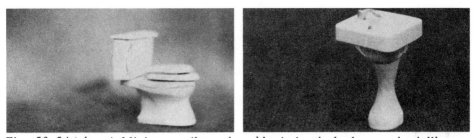

*Figs. 53–54 (above). Miniature toilet and washbasin for the bathroom of a dollhouse, which I made to standard 1:12 scale and painted white. Toilet seat and cover are hinged.*

*Figs. 55–56 (above and on next page). These miniature cabinet-making tools and portable tool chest, all usable, were made by the same craftsman who built the colonial shop model. Closed, the chest is the size of a cigarette pack so scale is about 1:12.*

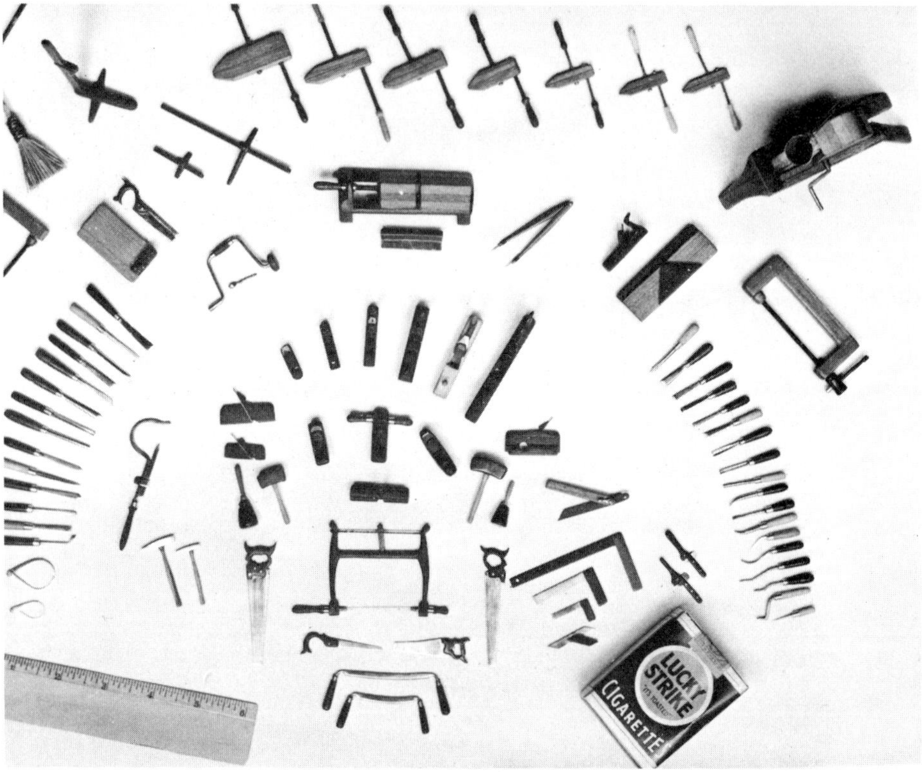

*Fig. 56.*

*Figs. 57–59. Farrier's shop and, on opposite page, sculptor's house and travelling magic show—three of a number of models made from hollow tree trunks by my grandson Robin at age 14–16. Scale is less than 1:12.*

*Fig. 58.*

*Fig. 59.*

## CHAPTER VII
# A Typical Model – an Ancient Barn

THE LADY HAD CHAIRED A COMMITTEE that raised funds to dismantle a Dutch-style barn built around 1690 and re-erect it on the grounds of our local historical society. In the process, she acquired a section of one of the original supports, a baulk of pine about 11 in (28 cm) square by 20 in (50 cm) long. Her question: What could I make of it to produce a memento? It was checked on one face and had a notch for a crossbrace near one end; also, it was rough and angled at the top.

First, I considered a Revolutionary soldier. He was 80 years too late for the barn. The same applied to profiles of Washington, Jefferson and Hamilton on the wide faces. A Dutch sailor of the period? An Indian? Neither was right. Then I came upon the idea of making a model of the barn on the end.

The original was about 24 × 41 ft (7.3 × 12.5 m), 16 ft (4.9 m) high at the eaves, and 8 ft (2.5 m) more from plate to ridge. Side bays 10 ft

*Fig. 60. The Sands barn after re-erection. It is 24 × 41 ft (7 × 12.5 m) and 16 ft (2 m) high at the eaves, with a 45° roof pitch. Of the Dutch type, it was built about 1690.*

(3 m) wide had been added, then removed at least 150 years ago. I found I could carve a barn on the rough end at approximately 1:50 scale, and have a good base remaining. The barn was angled slightly on the base, just to avoid rigidity, and the base was sloped, as it had been on the original barn to provide storage areas under the floor. The barn could be sawed to shape, and this provided wood for trim. Bits of soft iron wire could be hammered into hinges, door handles and other appurtenances. Grooving to simulate the vertical siding could be done easily with a V-tool, but what about the shingling?

At that point, I decided to whittle a miniature colonist actually shingling

*Fig. 61. The completed model, about 1:50 scale, is carved on the end of a support-post section of the original. The shingles, even older, are of 8,500-year-old Virginia cedar.*

the roof. In those remote days, barn shingles would be made of hand-split cedar, about 2 ft (61 cm) long. I had a piece of Virginia cedar from a marl pit at the "Blue Hole" near Castalia, Ohio, identified by the Forest Products Lab at Madison, Wisconsin, as *Juniperus Virginiana*, and by carbon-14 tests at the Institute for Nuclear Studies at the University of Chicago as 8500 years old, plus or minus 500 years. Thus, the tree grew just after glacial Lake Lundy receded from the area.

Other wood covered at the same time had rotted away hundreds of years ago, but the cedar was as sound as the day it was covered. What could be more appropriate for shingles? So I violated scale and split and shaved about 500 shingles of various widths about ⅜ in (9.6 mm) long—about 20:1 scale. (Random widths are not hard to achieve; they occur by breakage during splitting, just as they did 300 years ago.)

During the tedious shingle-making, I had time to research the process, with the result that I added two more colonists, one splitting the shingles and the other shaving them. For the splitting, a sawn block roughly 1 × 1 × 2 ft (30 × 30 × 60 cm) was wedged into a natural vise formed by a tree crotch over a stone base. Slabs of the desired thickness were split off with a frow (also spelled froe, and called a fromard or rending axe in England), a wide blade about 14 in (35.5 cm) long, with a haft extending back from the blade at one end. A frow club drove the frow into the baulk, then the handle was rocked back and forth to extend the split the length of the block. Wastage was high, but narrow sections were salvaged for fitting and capping.

Shingle blanks were clamped one by one on a shaving horse, so the edges could be cut true and one end thinned. The clamping arm was an adjustable lever (to take various wood thicknesses for various operations), weighted at the lower end and held by the operator's foot on a pedal. At the upper end was a large clamping headblock (called the "blockhead," of course), which held the shingle against the pull of the knife. (In Pennsylvania Dutch country, the drawknife was called a *Schnitzel* and the shaving horse a *Schnitzelbank*—hence the popular *Bierstube* song line, "Ist das nicht ein Schnitzelbank?")

Shingles were applied to solid boards or furring strips, either with nails or wooden pegs. I assumed this builder was wealthy enough to afford hand-forged nails, so the shingler could use a claw hammer (which dates back at least to ancient Rome!) rather than a wooden maul for pegs.

The three men and their appurtenances were carved of jelutong, which is a bit anachronistic. I also made their tools of aluminum, likewise anachronistic, but not so quick to oxidize as iron and appropriately colored to resemble used tools. Two of the three men are seated, and are about ¾ in (1.9 cm) tall overall. Each is dressed in appropriate costume, varying in carved details and tinted with oils. The man on the roof, sitting sidewise on his foot (Fig. 62), is the tricky one.

I provided him with appropriate ladders, one of the familiar present-day type, the other the old single-rail type, now rarely seen except for firemen's scaling ladders. They are lighter and easier to handle than a normal ladder and they hook to the roof peak; they were used primarily to bring supplies and to steady the shingler if the roof pitch was steep. Ladder rails are maple, drilled for rungs whittled from toothpicks. Shingles were glued in place singly and marked where necessary to suggest nails. The nameplate is a cross-section of a holly branch, with plain incised lettering darkened for easy reading.

Results of the research were typed on small pages, including a description of the history of the barn, and put in a hinged box that fit exactly into the old notch at the base. The owner plans eventually to enclose the barn in a circular vitrine, which will be the base of a glass-topped coffee table.

*Figs. 62–63. A closer view, showing froe-splitting at left and drawknife shaving at right. Note differences in costuming. Trim is of the original wood; hardware is hammered iron wire.*

# CHAPTER VIII

# A Cruiser in Action

### A "lifeless" moored boat can become something much more alive

INEVITABLY, SOME CARVINGS, PARTICULARLY MODELS, almost demand components of other materials. This project is such a case, a proposed gift for the owner of a 28-ft (8.5-m) cruiser. It could have been a scale model, an in-the-round carving, a panel, or almost anything else. The model would not just be a woodcarver's job; it would have too many metal fittings and a fiberglass hull. An in-the-round carving would be, in effect, a model devoid of some of the fittings, and likely to be somewhat static as well. My solution was a panel of the boat at high speed, coming almost head-on, so practically none of the deck fittings and similar hardware are visible. However, this introduces the problems of bow waves and wake, which for such a boat are mostly foam, and of a distorted perspective.

When the project was first discussed, I saw the boat and took a number of photographs, both of it and of an oil painting which included it. All were static to me. However, we did find a catalog that provided deck cross-sections

*Fig. 64. Bertram 28-ft (8.5-m) cruiser before a storm, a 1¾ × 12 × 18-in (4 × 30 × 46-cm) medium-relief plaque in butternut with music-wire rails. Finish is varnish, spray matte or satin, with Kiwi® shoe polish (neutral on hull and people, brown on background and sea).*

Figs. 65–67. Photos taken for details; note the many fittings, which would clutter up a woodcarving. Only the horns (whittled maple dowel, silvered) and rails are included in the carving. (Bottom photo courtesy Bertram Yacht Company, Miami, Florida.)

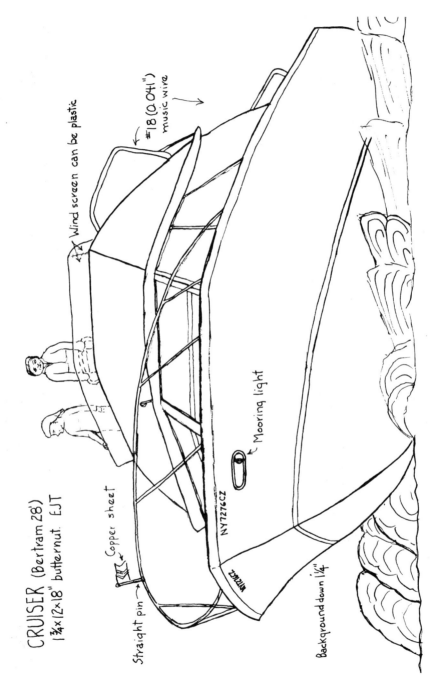

CRUISER (Bertram 28')
1¾×12×18" butternut. EJT

Wind screen can be plastic

#18 (0.041") music wire

Copper sheet

Straight pin

Mooring light

NY7276CZ

NY7276CZ

Background down 1¼"

Fig. 68.

and a 2 × 2½-in (5 × 6.4-cm) color photograph that suggested the present pose. I enlarged the silhouette by the point-to-point method (*see* Appendix II) to fit a piece of butternut I had, assuming that, when the time came, I'd be able to solve the problem of the waves, and that either music wire (tempered steel) or silver wire would form the visible portions of the rails. Whether or not the wind screen would be plastic like the original was also a moot question.

The accompanying step-by-step pictures (Figs. 69 to 76) show my solutions, some of them compromises. I tried the waves in various forms and techniques, and ultimately simply stylized them. I added a front block to make the boat project still more from the background, and I decided upon music wire rather than silver because of its greater stiffness and resistance to casual mistreatment. Teak or walnut would have been a better wood, particularly for the figures—except their color would probably have been too dark. Pine or basswood would have been too soft, at least in my opinion. There is no tinting or color.

## Step-by-step carving of the cruiser

(**Fig. 69**) A point-to-point sketch was made of 2 × 2½-in (5 × 6.5-cm) catalog picture to provide this pattern; pictures I could take were of necessity only details. The panel is butternut, 1¾ × 12 × 18 in (4.5 × 30 × 46 cm), with a bit of the scrap glued on to extend the top of the hull where it bulges, thus effectively increasing the panel depth to 2¼ in (5.7 cm).

(**Fig. 70**) An hour's roughing with ¼- and ½-in (6.3 and 12.7-mm) firmers and a 1-in (2.5-cm) flat spade gouge, produced this blank. Background was lowered 1¼ in (3 cm) on a tentative basis, and left with gouge marks plainly visible. Fortunately, grain was largely parallel with the surface. so only in one or two spots (upper left, for example) was it necessary to change the direction of the cut.

(**Fig. 71**) Experimental cutting was done to create some sort of wave form. because the spray actually resulting from the passage of a cruiser at speed is impossible to convert to solid lines. Original form was a deckled irregular surface (left), but this looks more and more like a mushroom or a sponge now. Tools are ⅛- and ¼-in (3.2- and 6.3-mm) gouges and a veiner.

(**Fig. 72**) The later wave form on the right is a simple series of loops suggesting the solid part of the waves created, with little effort to simulate spray. The hull shape was also refined and the decision made to retain the glued-on portion, at least for the time being.

*Fig. 69.*

*Fig. 70.*

*Fig. 71.*

*Fig. 72.*

(**Fig. 73**) Getting the proper slope and angle to the superstructure is an exercise in forced perspective. This is *not* an in-the-round carving, so the third dimension must be foreshortened. In this case, the superstructure cannot be carried all the way back to the background at the left (as viewed) because this would not allow enough wood for the female figure, and the forward slope of the front of the boat must be faked as well. This can be done by eye, using the right front (as viewed) of the superstructure as the high point. It was finished with firmer and flat gouge.

(**Fig. 74**) How close the left-hand edge of the superstructure can come to the background depends upon the female figure on that side. I carved her practically against the background and with her right hand resting on the windscreen (which determines its location and slope exactly), then sloped other surfaces in accordance. She is in partial profile, which adds complications, particularly in carving the face so close to the background, but the male is full-face, which makes only the ears a problem. Figures were done with knives.

(**Fig. 75**) A power cruiser is extensively decorated with chrome-plated gadgetry: vents, funnels, chocks, mooring lights, rails and stairways all over the place. In this "pose," most of the deck appurtenances are fortunately not visible, but the rails are, and in forced perspective at that. With an action picture (Fig. 67) as a guide, the railings could be distorted to suit. I began with the simple ones at the stern, and left the main rail until last. Almost all of the metal work here is #18 music wire (0.041 in [1 mm] diameter), which is stiff and difficult to cut, but will stay in position once it has been placed. The burgee is copper mounted on a straight pin, which in turn is bent around the rail and glued with "magic" glue, as are the joints of the supports. To reduce bulk, the wire is flattened before being formed into the loops on the supports.

(**Fig. 76**) The background was too light and patterned, and the block glued on the front was visible, so I "antiqued" some areas with teak stain, and accented the background darkness with brown Kiwi®shoe polish, using neutral Kiwi on the rest. This provides the low gloss I prefer. If the dark polish is applied and then wiped off before it dries, it will create darker edges and lines to generate the "antique" effect. The twin horns are whittled from dowel rod and silvered. The only other decorations are the twin white chevrons on the burgee, which otherwise is a natural copper color. (The club burgee is dark red and white anyway, so copper is close, and is less artificial against the background brown.

*Fig. 73.*

*Fig. 74.*

*Fig. 75.*

*Fig. 76.*

## CHAPTER IX
# Carve a House "Portrait"

### A photo or sketch provides the pattern; textures add realism

BUILDINGS, EITHER HOMES OR HISTORIC STRUCTURES, have a special appeal for most of us. What's more, they can be depicted relatively easily in a panel carving—if one starts with the right view. If you have a photograph or a detailed sketch of the building facade, that can serve for a low-relief pattern. What's more, a photograph usually incorporates the necessary perspective so that difficult and tedious task is avoided. The photo or sketch can be enlarged to the desired size by photostat or point-to-point drawing to get the basic outline, which is what you need to start. With a head-on view, perspective problems are minimized and outlines are usually square. If the building is set in bare surroundings, you may want to add a tree or two, some shrubbery, etc., and to strip it of such unsightly excrescences as TV antenna, telephone and electric lines, and even such difficult elements as porch railings, if they contribute little to the design. All such elements are difficult to carve. Greenery is not easy either, but it can be conventionalized or stylized.

*Fig. 77. Historic Broadstairs in Ghent, New York, is 250 years old with walls of Yonkers trap rock nearly 2 ft (.61 m) thick. This plaque portrait of it is 2 × 12 × 19-in (5 × 30 × 48-cm) Oregon sugar pine. Background is lowered 1 in (2.5 cm), while house ends are ½ in (12.7 mm) below the surface at left and almost ¾ in (19.5 mm) at right. Finish is matte varnish followed by antiquing with teak oil stain.*

To carve a structure in perspective is somewhat more difficult, of course, because lines that otherwise would be horizontal, angle to vanishing points at either side of center—and the vanishing points may be out far enough that drawing some of the lines will be difficult, let alone carving them so they look right. I have in this instance, however, undertaken such a plaque as a step-by-step project, to illustrate the method. A carving like this will provide excellent practice in two directions—one of carving in perspective, the other in achieving surface textures that appear realistic.

Obviously, you will want to select your own subject for depiction, so only the method will be detailed here. I chose as my building a historic posting inn in Ghent, New York, once called Broadstairs. It was built over 250 years ago by a Dutchman named Hoggeboom, and legend has it that he used to ride his horse up the front steps into the hall on Saturday nights, when he was the worse for wear. The house is fieldstone and has walls of Yonkers traprock about 2 ft (61 cm) thick. It is set on a slight eminence well back from the road. I took several photographs of it and selected one taken from the left-hand front corner. Because the house it set high, the camera lens was at the level of the house basement or below it, so all perspective is above center; the ground line is practically horizontal, while the roof lines are in high perspective. Note how the windows in the end gable are sloped, while first-floor windows are almost level with the base.

The house originally had a fireplace in every room, so it has five chimneys, three of which are visible. The walls are laid up roughly in courses, odd sections of stone being set in to maintain the lines. (Actually, relatively flat stone surfaces are achieved on interior and exterior courses, with rubble filling between them.) The big trees in the foreground at each side are maples, while the shrubbery is mostly evergreens, two trimmed vertical yews flanking the front door. Chimneys are brick.

Tools are indicated step by step—at least the ones I used. The wood was Oregon sugar pine, $2 \times 12 \times 18$ in $(5 \times 30 \times 46$ cm). I decided to make the drawing directly on the wood, and enlarged the photograph by the point-to-point method, including window and door locations. I had no later use for the drawing, so I did not make it on paper first; you may prefer to have a drawing of exact size for reference. It is convenient, by the way, to enlarge from the photograph in direct ratio. I had a $3 \times 5$-in $(7.5 \times 12.5$-cm) print and enlarged it exactly three times. I left framing branches on both sides, stylizing them to soften the edges of the carving.

*Fig. 78. This photo, along with a close-up, provided the basic pattern and shows detail of rear shed and far-side porch. Flanking trees were stylized in the carving and modified to obscure less of the building; they soften the house ends and amplify the illusion of perspective in the finished piece. Base planting was also modified slightly for clarity and front-step railing was eliminated. If added, the railing could be formed of music wire set into drilled holes.*

## Step-by-step carving of a house "portrait"

(**Fig. 79**) The sketch should be strengthened on the outer outlines to guide in the grounding-out. The depth of carving is somewhat arbitrary. I decided in this instance to lower the background 1 in (2.5 cm) and to self-frame the carving. Setting-in the lines is not too vital because any crushing of the upper fibres will be cut away anyhow, including the edges of the foliage swags. (Foliage swags are stylized from those in the photo to reduce the obscuring of the house and to permit convenient carving of the background.) Only major outlines are necessary at this juncture. To permit the house corner itself to be at the surface, small blocks were glued on at the eave and for the corner bush at the base. These simplify carving and give a desirable projection to the near point of the finished piece. Bosting was done with ⅛-, ¼-, and 1-in (3.2-, 6.3-, and 25.4-mm) flat gouges, ¼-in (6.3-mm) round gouge and ⅛-, ¼-, and ½-in (3.2-, 6.3-, and 12.7-mm) firmers. Depth was checked with a machinist's 6-in (15-cm) scale with a slider that could be set to 1 in (2.5 cm). (Any pin with a 1-in (2.5-cm) mark on it will do, but the scale is convenient.

*Fig. 79.*

*Fig. 80.*

(**Fig. 80**) A photo flattens perspective, so if relief is to be unusually high, the sketch must be modified from the photo, depending upon the depth of relief. (If the house were in the round, all dimensions would be true to scale instead of foreshortened; this would be nearly true of very high relief as well.) When carving the sloping side and front, the dimensions of windows and other details must be carried in from the surface *vertically*, so I carved around each to get the desired slope to the wall—about ½ in/8 in (1.3/20 cm), or $\frac{1}{16}$ in/1 in (1.6 mm/25.4 mm). If the depth at the edges were to be increased to several times that, the widths of windows and other details would have to be increased from those in the photograph to gain a realistic effect. Some care must be used in setting-in to maintain vertical sides. To maintain a constant slope on the end wall, begin by carving the desired slope on the portion of the wall between first- and second-floor windows, which is unobstructed, then work outward from this base. Tools must be kept very sharp, and can be the same as those for grounding-out, plus a knife for tight corners.

(**Fig. 81**) Once the general wall surface is carved, window surfaces can be cut back to the same slope. Remember to allow wood for the projecting sill and capital on each window, as well as for the eaves of the house itself. Eaves can be shaped and chimneys cut back to shape, then scored to suggest bricks. (I actually carved vees with a knife to outline bricks, which is perhaps excessive detail.) A V-tool can be used for some of this, but it is likely to tear wood across grain unless it is unusually sharp at the tip. Window mullions are not projections, but V-grooves. You can show sash outlines, of course, but such detail is unnecessary.

(**Fig. 82**) The front is roughed in the same manner as the end wall was. It is more complex than the side, particularly at the outer end, where contouring is deep and windows are small and close together. Also, the central pillar of the front door and the decorative windows over it make it impossible to get a continuous surface except at the eave. Immediately cut down the level of the windows at far right for tool clearance, unless you have short-bent tools. Allow extra width at a major projection like the front door to get later slope and moldings depicted on it, as well as a small porch and simulated steps in front. (I abandoned the stair rail as unnecessary and not particularly attractive.) I worked out varying textures for the nearby trees and for the bushes, actually carving stylized maple leaves on the tree areas and using gouged surfaces with enhancing lines on the bushes, all done with fluter and veiner. The flared capitals on the windows can be carved originally,

*Fig. 81.*

*Fig. 82.*

(**Fig. 83**) Note the difference in the widths of the left and right windows caused by perspective, also the difference in the heights of the yews flanking the porch, which in actuality are alike in size and position. In this case, the photograph is the best guide for perspective. Once wall and window slopes are attained, details can be carved, including various capitals on columns and moldings. The far-right window has been antiqued; compare the effect. Note dentate molding under the eaves and over the door. Texturing of the yew is done with a V-tool, cutting out small chips. Maple leaves are an approximation of 5-lobed leaves, much larger than scale. The wall is textured, as are the porch steps and other elements. The carving was not sanded. It was given two coats of spray matte varnish to seal end-grain areas and avoid stain buildup there. Then a teak oil stain was painted over the surface and immediately wiped off with a cloth, so it is retained largely in depressions. Final surfacing was to polish with neutral shoe polish.

*Fig. 83.*

*Figs. 84–85. A different approach to scenic portraiture is this Brazilian panel by Alvaro Mariana. It is 5 × 22-in (13 × 56-cm) mahogany and antique-stained. The shape is unusual, as are the textured details. It has no border and suggests much greater width than it has, particularly because of the irregular top and side. This carver has made a number of other vignettes in like proportion.*

# CHAPTER X

# Likenesses of Pets

## Dogs and horses are popular subjects

MANY PEOPLE WHO HAVE PETS OR FAVORITE ANIMALS are interested in having likenesses, not of the breed or species, but of their particular favorite, particularly if that favorite is getting old. And animals are as individual as humans when you study them; each varies a little from the norm, and the owner or admirer is very conscious of those variations.

I remember two of my early attempts at likenesses of animals almost 50 years ago. One was an Arabian mare, the other a bulldog, and I pictured them in my first book, *Whittling and Woodcarving* (Dover), in 1936. In each case the owner provided profile pictures or the equivalent, but I learned that it requires several photographs, and preferably a chance to study the animal, if you are going to get a likeness that will satisfy the proud admirer. What's more, an animal anatomy book will provide you with some basic understanding of skeleton and musculature, which photographs often obscure because of the lighting or the animal's pelt.

I have reproduced these early likenesses here. "Honey Girl" (Fig. 89) was in mahogany and mounted on walnut. Note how the grain helped show the swell of the neck. "Bill" (Fig. 90) was also in mahogany and similarly mounted. Both had leather additions, the harness finished with silver buckle and snaffle, and the collar a section of an actual dog collar with brass name-plate and chain. I think the leather harness added something, but the dog collar was a bit overpowering, and I'm fairly certain that if either carving is still extant, the leather trim has rotted away. No trim, or a carved harness or collar from the solid, would have been better. Both were, however, finished with low gloss, of which I'm proud.

In this chapter are additional examples of dogs, which are the most popular subjects. The female St. Bernard (Fig. 88) is in the round, and desk-size, 6 in (15 cm) long, finished with oils, while the setter panel (Fig. 100) is natural-finish except for the darkened or antiqued background. The setter was carved by a student who previously had used the knife almost exclusively, while this carving was done mostly with palm gouges.

Although a St. Bernard and a schnauzer (Figs. 88 and 95) should be relatively alike in difficulty, hence in time to carve, I found the latter twice as difficult. One factor was size, another the wood, and hence the texture and finish. I had photographs of both dogs, and each pattern had to be a composite of elements in several photographs. But the schnauzer, cowed by the camera, never did strike the basic "show" pose of the breed that his mistress wanted; I had to adapt that from a magazine picture of another dog. Also, he had normal ears, not lopped ones, and he carried both ears and tail down because of his concern over the photography. I decided on myrtle wood because of its grey-white color, very much like that of the dog, instead of painted white pine or basswood, so that added complications. As completed, the carving required only a slight tinting around the jowls to get the characteristic head coloration and likeness, and is much more realistic, yet natural, than the St. Bernard portrait.

## MAMSELLE - Female long-haired St. Bernard — Basswood

*Figs. 86–88. Mamselle, a female St. Bernard, was carved in basswood and painted with oils. Some knife lines were left and some paint rubbed thin to retain the idea of wood. Figure 87 shows one of a series of photos I took to get the lifted foot and tail the owner wanted. Dog was carved integrally with base, which was then appliquéd on a rosewood base block.*

*Fig. 87.*

*Fig. 88.*

*Fig. 89. I carved this mahogany-on-walnut portrait of Honey Girl, a prize-winning Arab mare, over 40 years ago. Harness is cut from thin leather and fittings are silver.*

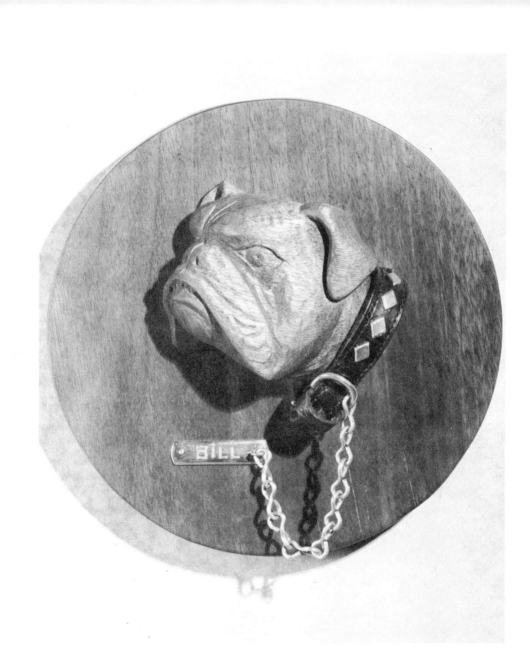

*Fig. 90. Bill was an aging bulldog. I carved him from mahogany and, again, used a walnut base for mounting. Collar is a section of a real one chained to the brass plaque with a screweye. The head is about 3 in (8 cm) tall.*

In any likeness of a pet, you must be conscious not only of the visual distinctions to your untrained eye, but also to the real or imagined distinctions that the owner sees, particularly those he or she considers important. Thus a schnauzer is supposed to have a hollow under his belly that accentuates his chest curvature, coloration around the muzzle, a definite goatee line around the mouth, a forward and alert pitch of the ears, a straight back and multiple-curved hind-leg line, etc.

These elements are essential to a likeness because the client sees his animal ideally. You, as a stranger, will rarely see all these things together, and are even less likely to capture them in photographs. Also, photos are two-dimensional; you have a third dimension to recreate, usually by trial and error. In this case, the block was half of the original 7-in-diameter (17.5-cm) trunk, so I had to guess at the proper thickness to saw the blank.

The schnauzer has a more complex head shape than the St. Bernard, and the difference in wood is also a delaying factor. But the major expenditure of extra time was in the meticulous texturing of the dog's pelt, which was done with small veiner and fluter and took almost a day and a half. The eyes, set deeply behind shaggy brows, and the feathery character of the lower legs, also took extra time to achieve.

*Figs. 91–93. Rarely will one photograph depict exactly the personality and peculiarities of a particular animal. The one above shows body shape and proper ear pose, while two on opposite page provide eye and mouth details.*

*Fig. 92.*

*Fig. 93.*

Figs. 94–95. *Myrtle gave coloration quite close to the dog's, while touching up nose tip with black, eyes with brown and eyebrows and face hair with gray (below) created a recognizable and individual portrait. White pigment was also tipped on feathery hairs of lower legs.*

I mention all these things to draw the contrast between a likeness and a simple depiction. It is reinforced by the low-relief head of the same dog I carved from the remainder of the slab of myrtle—about 6 × 6 × 1 in (15 × 15 × 2.5 cm) at its thickest (Fig. 98). This head was laid out by eye alone (no laborious squares or point-to-point), sawed to a rough silhouette, and shaped with a ½-in (12.7-mm) flat gouge while held to the bench with a carver's screw. The rough shape of the head was achieved in about an hour, and the head was finished with smaller gouges and a V-tool in a few hours more, or less than a fourth of the time required for the scaled likeness.

Perhaps to anyone except the owner, the head is as dramatic and interesting as the full dog, even though its proportions are not exact. The left eye, for example, is set too deeply, texturing is rough and only suggestive, and the mouth and nose are not detailed. These examples emphasize the differences between a quick study and a portrait.

*Figs. 96–98 (above and on next page). Here is another recognizable study of the dog, this one a caricature rather than a likeness. Eyes, eyebrows and nose are emphasized; face hair is only suggested. Because this is low relief rather than in-the-round, some contours must be accentuated and others played down as seen in the next two stages of carving. Note knot in center of forehead and check running down nose from it. Both were filled with glue and sawdust, then sanded and tinted to match adjacent wood (Fig. 98).*

Fig. 97.

Fig. 98.

*Figs. 99–100. Walnut panel of Ludi, a seven-year-old Irish Setter, is ¾ × 11 × 12 in (1.9 × 28 × 30 cm) overall. It was carved by Hugh Minton, Jr., of Aiken, South Carolina. Much of the carving and all of the texturing was done with palm tools; background was then antiqued with walnut stain to make the head stand out.*

## CHAPTER XI

# Catch Your Own Trout

## Action poses and the "wavelet" problem

THIRTY YEARS OR MORE AGO, I CARVED A TROUT IN BASSWOOD, tinted him, and mounted him on a chaste disk of walnut. That carving came to mind when a friend asked me to do a leaping trout for his fishing club. We agreed on walnut, partly because I had an air-dried log 7 in (17.5 cm) in diameter and relatively free of checks. I would use a largely vertical pose as I had done earlier, with the leader of a real fly caught around the trout's tail.

So far, so good. But what about the water? Anyone who has ever caught a trout knows that when he leaps there is more spray than water around him, and any woodcarver knows that spray and clouds are the most difficult elements to portray in carved wood. This time I couldn't evade the problem by mounting the fish, because we both wanted an action pose, so I had to achieve something that was definitely water and spray, if it couldn't be a likeness.

The best answer I've found is to stylize the water in one way or another, as I did in carving the cruiser (Chapter 8), and as the Japanese have done for some hundreds of years in their temple carvings of sacred carp (see Fig. 104). They depict water as a sinuous, stylized wave, with small and elaborate curls along its upper surface to suggest spray.

In my carving, the fish had to appear practically free of the water and yet be supported by it, so I designed him as if he'd just delivered a mighty tail-slap to the surface to free himself of the snagged hook.

The carving is shown in the step-by-step photographs (Figs. 105 to 109). It was such a success with the client's family, all ardent anglers, that they insisted upon keeping it themselves. I made another one, quite similar, for the club, and three smaller ones, all in walnut and in various poses, for the children. Note the differences in shape and tail formation between a rainbow and a German brown (Figs. 101 and 102), and in fin positions, depending upon the position of the fish. They are as accurate as I could get them from available references. They had to be likenesses of particular kinds, because the recipients knew the differences, in both color and shape.

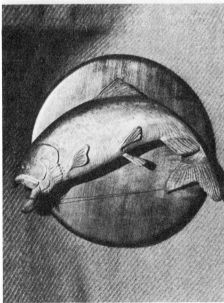

*Figs. 101–103. Rainbow and German brown trout (top left and right) in walnut, 7 × 7 × 15 in (18 × 18 × 38 cm), are each one piece except for right dorsal fin and artificial fly. Both are adapted from the 30-year-old painted basswood rainbow carving at left. Note differences in tail and mouth shapes between the two upper carvings and the painted original.*

Fig. 104. Stylized waves in the Japanese fashion in keyaki (zelkova wood), which resembles elm and has a distinctive grain. Fish are carp—note the large scales.

Fig. 105 (left). Rough out portion of the fish above splash level with a carpenter's saw, allowing added thickness for twist in upper body. Portions near base are split out and shaped with a 1-in (2.5-cm) gouge and flat chisel. Fig. 106 (right). Upper body is rough-shaped with 1¼-in (3.2-cm) carpenter's gouge and 1½-in (3.8-cm) low-sweep spade gouge, with block held by carver's screw on a bench edge. Rough outlines of fins are put in with fluter and ¼- and ½-in (6.3- and 12.7-mm) deep gouges. Note early shaping of wave and tail areas.

*Fig. 107 (left). Templates of stiff cardboard guide in body shaping and in positioning of elements.*

*Fig. 108 (above). Tail elements are now shaped and fins defined and fluted. A double row of wavelets in an irregular pattern was developed, with minor undercutting. One-fourth- and ⅝-in (6.3- and 16-cm) low-sweep gouges, veiner, V-tool and several medium-sweep gouges of various widths were used to attain variety in wavelet shape.*

*Fig. 109 (left). Wavelets rise higher in back, since a trout hitting the surface would cause such a pattern. White growth wood in back was carefully retained to suggest spray. Right ventral fin did not project sufficiently and was replaced by a separate fin.*

*Figs. 110–112. Three smaller poses, each about 6 in (15 cm) on the longest dimension, were carved in the same way as the two larger ones. Two have conventional waves because the fish are leaving the water; the third at bottom right has ripples because the fish is entering. Trout above has just shaken the hook loose so, instead of on a leader, fly is held on a shaped thin-diameter music wire. Tool marks remain on each, showing they are unmistakably wood, hand-carved. Finish is oil and wax, with a top coat of Kiwi® neutral shoe polish to heighten gloss.*

*Figs. 113–114. These two fish offer contrast. At right the important likeness is not the minnow but the hand, which must look realistic and capable. This one was carved by M. Paul Ward in 1972 from a design of mine over 40 years old. The fish at bottom is a stylized Japanese concept of a carp in pine, about 2 × 6 × 15 in (5 × 15 × 38 cm). I made it in three hours out of curiosity when I found it advertised in a mail-order catalog for $150. Finish is selective staining and matte varnish because the carving hangs outside.*

# CHAPTER XII
# Why Not Carve a Mask?

A MAN'S FACE IS MUCH MORE THAN HIS FORTUNE; it is the best visible clue to who and what he is, and the focus of every other man's (and woman's) eye. Thus, it is not at all surprising that we ascribe certain characteristics to certain faces, identify famous or infamous personages by real or fancied facial characteristics, or imagine specific faces for our particular idols and gods.

Man has carved faces to represent animals, birds, gods and humans, or to picture his fears and his fancies, since well before the dawn of history. The ancient Greeks, Chinese, Koreans, Indonesians, Japanese, Inca, Maya, Maori, Eskimos, American Indians, and all the races of Europe made and used them in plays, even worshipped them as the personification of their gods. The Africans and Melanesians still make them for ancestor worship, cult dances, and for instructing the young. They are also still made for dances in Bali, Java, Ceylon (Sri Lanka), Fiji, New Guinea, Mexico, Guatemala, and Haiti. They were made here by the Iroquois, Hopi, Zuni, Tewa, Klingit, Apache and other tribes. Even Switzerland, the Tyrol, Italy, England, Siberia and India had masks.

*Fig. 115. Monkey and two jaguar masks are typical of the miniatures now made frequently. The largest is about 3 in (8 cm) tall and all are painted. The jaguar's inserted bristles (center) are from a pig.*

African masks that come from a broad band across the center of the continent are perhaps the best known in the United States, as a result of tourist and decorator purchases. These include the most elaborate abstract ones, but strikingly unusual masks of a similar type are also carved in Haiti. Perhaps the finest and truest-to-life masks were the more than 100 designs of the Japanese Noh masks (*see* Chapter 13). Because of our mixed heritage, most Americans now think of masks only as something associated with children and Halloween.

All sorts of materials have been used for masks: metal (for warriors), stone (for mummies), shell, ivory, terra-cotta, bone, papier-mâché, canvas (ancient Greeks), as well as wood and combinations of the above with or without precious stones. But wood was and is the "old reliable." It is strong, relatively permanent, light and stable, takes detail and finishes well, and is not abrasive on the face if well finished inside. The usual woods are straight-grained and relatively soft, like our white pine and basswood, even balsa and ash. In Central America, they use copal and blanco, much like our white pine. In other countries, they use similar native woods, unless the mask is to be wall-mounted rather than worn, in which case better and more attractive woods may be used, without painting—mahogany, ebony, two-toned woods like Fijian *nawa-nawa*, you name it. I used myrtle for my Noh mask.

Primitive carvers add feathers, beads, shells, ivory, horsehair, bone, stones, hide, metals, glass, turtle shells, vegetable fibres, even human scalps. The pressures of tourism have resulted in the carving of miniature masks of all sizes to serve as decorations, doorpulls, buttons, knobs, cane tops, box and chest ornaments, pendants, and brooches. Masks with lights behind them can be quite dramatic wall decorations.

It is strange that so few American carvers have made masks, because they provide excellent training in face carving, particularly caricature. Furthermore, if they are not copies, they require the carver to study features and expressions, so he can depict such emotions as rage, fear, disdain, happiness, and devotion. Slight errors usually don't matter on a mask; they may even help. Proportions are usually not exact; the real challenge is to cut loose from diffident scraping into bold, strong cuts and lines, so shadows can do their work. Further, most masks cover only the front of the face, so there is no problem with locating ears, shaping the head, or even depicting hair. The primitive wearer uses his own ears or covers the head and ears with a cloth or other drape, headdress, or wig.

Eyes, on the other hand, are often very detailed on masks—reflecting my initial remarks about how other people always watch the face (and particularly the eyes) as a clue to what we are thinking. The mask wearer may see through slits or holes in the mask eyes or, if the shape is different, through slits cut in convenient areas. Because a mask tends to be slightly larger than the face to allow for wall thickness, holes or slits in the irises of the mask eyes will be misplaced, so actual viewing slits may be cut in the crease beneath the lower lid or, more commonly, in the crease between eyebrow and eye. Also, nostrils are pierced to make breathing within the mask a bit easier. In the case of grotesques or animal masks, placing sight holes may be extremely difficult.

Because a mask is often a caricature, sides do not have to balance; eyes and cheeks can be higher or lower, the mouth can be twisted—things that would not be done in a formal portrait. Also, because a great many masks are painted, slight miscuts or flaws can be corrected with gesso, plastic wood, or whatever. The primary need is to make bold, slashing cuts, even if they are slightly wrong, rather than to spend an eternity nibbling away to copy precisely some formal original. The masks shown here were selected largely with that idea in mind.

*Figs. 116–117 (above and on opposite page). Two views of life-size masks from the Oaxaca area of Mexico. They range from animals and demons to humans. Some are painted; all are wearable.*

Fig. 117.

Fig. 118 (above). Elaborate painted Mexican masks are each about 24 in (61 cm) tall. Both are intended for wall decorations but have hollowed backs. If worn, they would extend above the head.

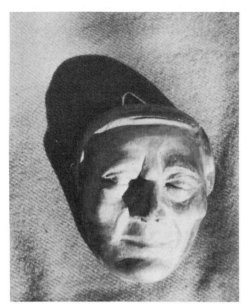

*Fig. 119 (left). Some masks are realistic. This one is the face of Benito Juarez, a hero to all Mexicans. It was made near Oaxaca and is neither painted nor tinted. It is of balsa!*

*Figs. 120–121 (below and right). Two versions of a demon mask, from Mexico. Mask below has articulated jaw, while the one at right is about 18 in (46 cm) high and extends down over wearer's chest. Both have viewing slits between eye bulge and brow.*

Figs. 122–123 (above and right). Demon, monkey and jaguar masks, the first in a colorful wood and the third, at right, painted. The first has an Oriental cast of features.

Fig. 124 (left). This Baule mask from Africa is an accurate likeness of a human face. Note that ears are included.

Whether or not a mask is to be worn, it should be hollowed out. This not only permits piercing of the eyes, nose and mouth, but it also makes the mask much lighter and less prone to checking and warping. The hollowing is best done after rough-carving of the features; the mass of wood inside provides a convenient means of anchoring the mask during roughing, and the rough outside shaping later provides a convenient guide for obtaining fairly uniform wall thickness. Hollowing is done with fairly large gouges, working alternately from top and bottom with the grain. It is advisable to hollow inside the nose, even if the mask is not to be worn, and to follow the cheek and brow contours to a degree.

Generally speaking, mask-making is a gouge job, not a knife job. Primitives usually do much of the shaping with an adz, particularly in Africa and British Columbia, the adz having a gouge-shaped blade for the roughing work in particular. Lines of the face, beard, tattoo marks, and hollowed areas are difficult with just the knife. Grain normally runs with the line of the nose, and complex elements which project very far, such as horns, a pointed nose or chin, or ears on animal masks, are carved separately and added, for both economy in wood and strength. Except for animal and some Noh masks, the ears are usually not included; they may, however, be represented by caricatured ones tacked on the mask edge, as is done on some Balinese masks. Much is made of such things as slanting eyes, crooked noses, heavy jaws, protruding teeth and tongues. (The Maori have a whole language based on tongue positions: straight out is a challenge, to one side is a welcome, a split tongue denotes a liar or deceiver, etc.) Sometimes, the nose is distorted or even symbolic, as in one New Guinea mask and several of the Haitian ones pictured (Figs. 126 and 127).

If wood equivalent to a half-log is not available, the blank can be built up in laminated layers. This also reduces wood cost and hollowing labor. Laminations cause no problems in a mask which is to be painted anyway. With modern 2-in (5-cm) planks, a simple way to gain thickness is to glue on a rough-formed nose blank, as well as brows and a chin tip if it suits the design.

Most mask designs are relatively realistic, but some African tribes and the Haitians excel at producing highly abstract masks with all sorts of symbolic decorations. These may violate most of the rules of facial proportion, and in fact may on occasion not resemble a face at all. Other peoples may extend the mask downward into a body, or upward into an elaborate headdress, or may distort the visage laterally or vertically. Some masks (African and Maori, for example) may even have two or three faces on them, one above another, either semi-realistic or abstract. Balinese masks simulate gods, based on some animal like a lion or a monkey, so they can become unbelievably fanciful and detailed. Many such masks, however, have become standardized through the years so they are readily recognized by natives as a particular character, evil or benevolent, even though they merely look like threatening demons to the unschooled Western eye.

Basically, a mask begins with wood large enough to fit the face of the wearer, plus perhaps ½ in (12.7 mm) all around for thickness. If there are other excrescences, allow extra wood, but don't overestimate the width necessary. Note that the mask will only fit back to the tops of the cheek-bones in most instances. This is narrower than the width in front of the ears, as I discovered when I made a Noh mask about 1 in (2.5 cm) too wide. Secondly, the mask will usually cover the chin, but need only be ¼ in (6.3 mm) thick at the point, and need not cover the entire forehead, which will usually be wigged or covered in some other way.

Saw the block to the rough mask outline, then hold it to the bench top with a carver's screw, screws or nails through a ¾-in (19-mm) baseboard into it, or on a bench hook. Mark the nose position and general shape, then slab off wood around it to get the general face contour. (This is easy if the nose block is laminated on top or if you start with a half-log.) Remember to leave wood for horns, ears, protruding eyes or chin, beard or moustache, and a possible hairline at the top. Also, the forehead is usually not cut as far back as the chin and cheeks.

Remember that the usual face, independently of the nose, is ovoid, like an upended egg. Rough out the cheeks and the hollows around the eyes. Locate and rough in the mouth, including the strong lines from the nostrils outward, unless they will be obscured by a grimace or a beard. Once you have the rough shape, remove the mask and hollow the inside. It can be held on the knees for this, or laid on a sand-filled leather cushion so the nose blank will not be damaged. (Don't hollow the nose yet; leave that for later or you may have a crushed nose.)

Once rough-hollowing is completed, the mask can be held over the knee, on a sand-filled cushion, or over a formed anchor block for finish-shaping. Lines like tattoos and facial blemishes can be depicted by grooves and hatching, of course, and general surfaces can be left as a series of small planes, unless you are trying to create the ultra-smoothness of a Noh mask or an actual portrait. Finishing should likewise be bold and stronger than life.

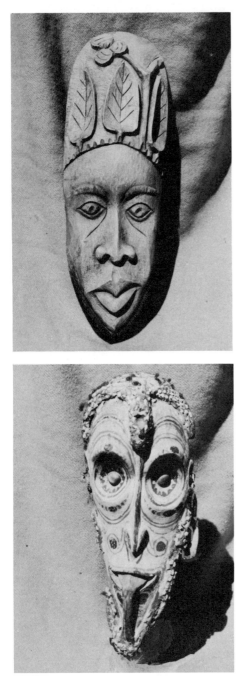

*Figs. 125–126 (top left and below). Haitian masks range from somewhat stylized and attenuated human faces to highly abstract depictions. One of these uses a lizard for nose, eyebrows and nose lines, another uses a palm tree. Mahogany is the usual wood—there is much of it around.*

*Fig. 127 (left). New Guinean masks tend to stress eyes and tongue. This one at left has stylized nose and tongue and a human scalp instead of hair. (Courtesy Dr. Roy Stephens.)*

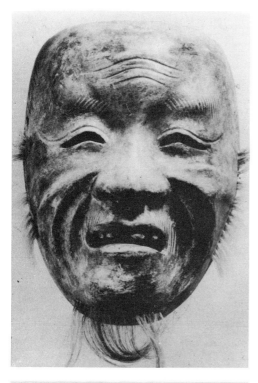

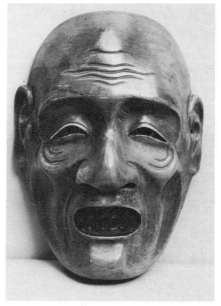

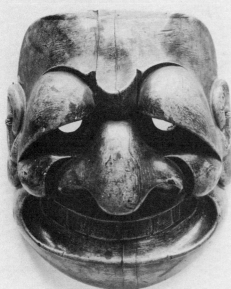

Figs. 128–130. Three Japanese masks
illustrate the craftsmanship of that
country's mask makers. Here are two
versions of an old man and one of a
demon, Obechima (left). Note that the
first two extend back to the ears.
(Courtesy Metropolitan Museum of Art,
New York City.)

## CHAPTER XIII
# Carve Your Own Noh Mask

THE JAPANESE ARE REPUTEDLY THE MOST ACCOMPLISHED makers of masks in the world, and the Noh mask is considered their finest. Thus, when I learned that a book had been published on how to make a half-dozen different types of Noh mask, I sent to Japan for a copy. This particular mask of an old priest (Fig. 131) intrigued me most in the book, so I decided to make it.

Step-by-step photographs and diagrams were plentiful in the book, and the basic dimensions were provided. The text was, of course, in Japanese, and it turned out that the dimensions given were neither in English nor metric, but in some sort of ratio. As I went along, I also found that two different masks had been used for the photographs, and they differed slightly in wrinkles and decoration. I discovered then that Confucius' remark about one picture being worth a thousand words is not literally true; there were times, in fact, when I'd have settled for the reverse.

This particular mask is normally made of a soft wood and finished with a glossy coat of off-white enamel, with tinting around the mouth and cheeks. I decided instead to make mine of myrtle and leave the natural finish. I also wanted it to fit me. I had half of an 8½-in (21-cm) log, which was thus 4¼ in (11 cm) at the center. Rough measurements of my face indicated that I needed a width of 7¾ in (19.7 cm) and a depth of 3¾ in (9.5 cm), allowing for ½-in (12.7-mm) walls. I decided to leave the additional width and depth and simply hollow the mask a bit deeper. The log half was also a bit longer than the original, but one does not waste myrtle, so I added to the forehead. None of these enlargements caused trouble, but I did find that when I got to the hollowing, I could have decreased the width by 1¼ in (3 cm), even for my wide face, with other dimensions correspondingly smaller. Therefore, I've put no dimensions on my sketches; you can fit your own face—remembering that you'll probably overestimate as I did. If you photostat the outside templates to ¾ in (19 mm) or 1 in (25 mm) wider than the width of your face at the cheekbone level, you should come out all right. All templates and sketches are in proportion to the basic half-outline you use first.

*Fig. 131. Old priest, a wearable Japanese Noh mask in myrtle, with movable lower jaw.*

## Carving the Noh mask, step by step

LAY OUT A VERTICAL CENTERLINE on both front and back of the piece. Lay out the basic mask shape on the flat back, using the template on both sides of the centerline. Figure 133 shows the layout, and how you can saw off the corners with a straight saw to shorten the heavy chisel work. When contour is achieved, cut off the outer edges of the front of the piece, if you started with a block, so you have a rough half-log shape. Then lay out the cross lines for the low spots *below* the brow, the nose and the lips, and begin to cut away the wood until you have achieved *almost* the desired depth (Fig. 134). Shape the face profile until the profile template fits along the centerline, then re-establish the basic vertical centerline (Fig. 135).

# JAPANESE NOH MASK

(Old priest, with movable jaw)

(This is a larger-than-life size. If it is to be worn, reduce scale)

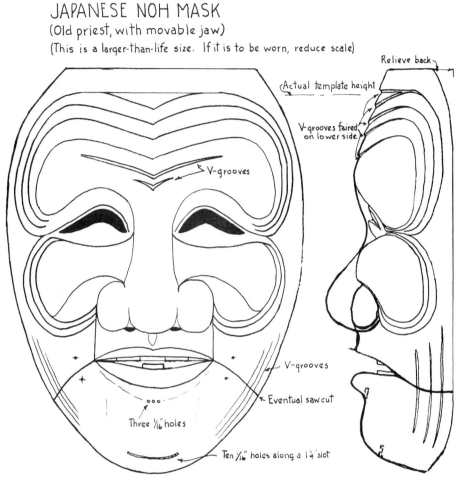

Relieve back

Actual template height

V-grooves faired on lower side

V-grooves

V-grooves

Eventual saw cut

Three 1/16" holes

Ten 1/16" holes along a 1¼" slot

*Fig. 132.*

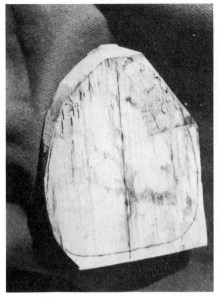

*Fig. 133.*

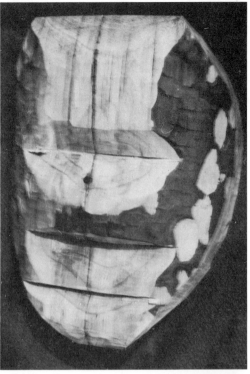

*Fig. 134.*

*Fig. 135.*

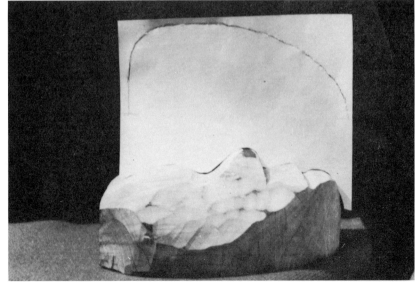

Begin to hollow around the eyes and nose, leaving the eyeball and cheek at their original level (Fig. 136). Note that the nose template goes across at the nostril line, and that the wood is *not* cut away above the nostrils nor at the outer edges. However, the wood *is* cut away at the outer edges beyond the lip template, which is almost an extended half-circle. It is also cut away outside the chin template. As you cut, refer to the photograph showing the templates in place (Fig. 137). At this point you can round off the sides of the mouth and chin and locate the mouth template and draw around it (Fig. 138).

At this stage, I decided to rough-hollow the interior, using straight and short-bent gouges. If you are holding the piece in a vise, be sure to leave plenty of wood at the outer edges to avoid breaking the side walls of the mask. You can also locate the eye and nostril positions and cut deeper at those points to simplify the next steps and make drilling and sawing easier (Fig. 139).

Now return to the face of the mask and achieve a rough face shape by defining the nostrils and shaping the eyeballs and cheeks. When this is completed, lay out the lines of the face and the eye slots according to the face pattern (Fig. 140). The decorative lines around the face are essentially V-slots, but they may be finished in various ways, according to what I could make out of the Japanese book. They may be V-slots with the sides faired so the areas between have a convex shape; they may simply be V-grooves with sharp edges; or one side of the V-groove may be eased or faired so they become the equivalent of teeth on a ratchet. This is what I did, starting at the center of the brow and on the lower edge of the groove (which becomes the upper edge at the sides of the eyes). Where the grooves meet at the sides of the eyes is roughly equivalent to switches in an old-fashioned railroad yard; study the full-face sketch carefully before you work on this area. The two short wrinkles at the center of the brow, by the way, are better as simple V-grooves, deep at the center and fading away to nothing as they move outward (Fig. 141).

It is also possible, at this point, to cut the lower jaw free. This is done with a scroll saw, and the cut is at right angles to the plane of the mask. Note that the cut enters at the points of the mouth outline, but passes above center to provide a fuller lower lip. This can be seen clearly in the side view of the mask (Fig. 142). Note also in this view how the cheeks and brows are faired into the lines, the chin shape, and the three decorative V-grooves on each side of the jaw.

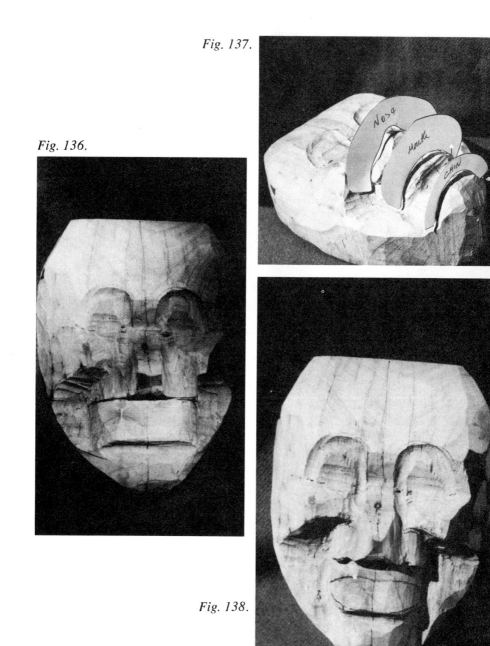

*Fig. 137.*

*Fig. 136.*

*Fig. 138.*

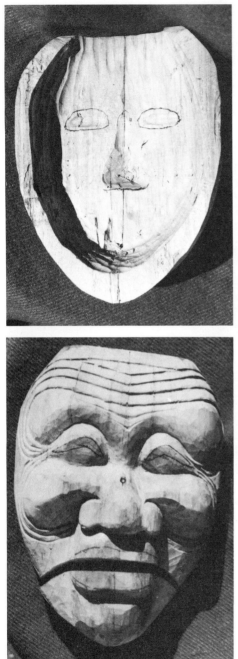

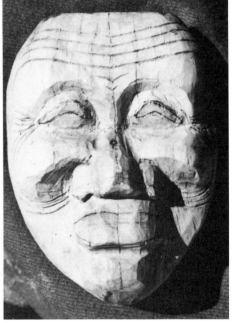

*Fig. 139.*

*Fig. 140.*

*Fig. 141.*

*Fig. 142.*

Now complete the shaping of the nostrils, cheeks, and eyes. Drill and saw out the eye slots and make any adjustments necessary at the back to thin the wood behind eyes and nostril holes. Note that there is a fine groove on the upper eyelid that suggests lashes, and a shallow groove over each eye near the bridge of the nose to accentuate the Oriental eye. (This is not sketched, to reduce complexity.) The eyeball shape is also strongly accented by grooves at top and bottom that flow into the wrinkle rings at the sides.

It is also possible now to shape the lips and teeth, the latter from the wood behind the lips (Fig. 143). For some reason, the priest has a single, centered lower tooth, which no human ever has, flanked by two upper teeth, all quite wide. These are shown clearly on the back and bottom photos of the sequence (Figs. 144 and 145). The holes for the jaw ties and side fastening may also be drilled at this point.

Essential work on the mask is now complete, but it will need some cleaning up and shaping, as well as decoration. The moustache is painted on—vertical stripes of black—but the beard is real. Three small holes are drilled about ⅜ in (9.6 mm) deep at the center base of the lower lip, and ten in line below the point of the chin, to take the beard hairs. The latter are set

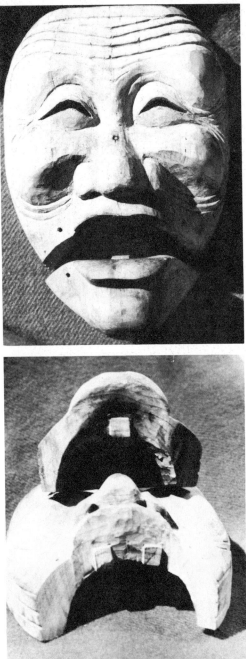

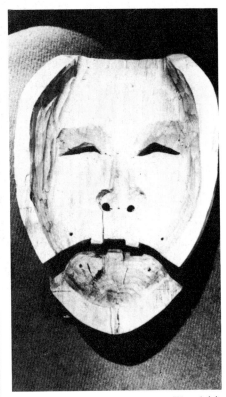

Fig. 143.

Fig. 144.

Fig. 145.

*Fig. 146.*

in a groove about $\frac{1}{16}$ in (1.6 mm) deep, which makes alignment easier and will conceal peg ends later. Horsehair is a good beard material; I used white hair from an old violin bow. Heavy thread or nylon filament could also be used, but I found 15 strands of horsehair per hole just about right. Suit length to your own fancy; I liked it about 9 in (22.5 cm) long, with ragged lower ends (Fig. 146). If you wet the ends of the horsehairs with a plastic cement, they will cling together and enter the hole quite easily. There they are anchored and spread with a driven-in plug behind them. This can be made from a toothpick or splinter of pine. The rosettes at each side of the forehead are about 1½ in (4 cm) in diameter. They are made from fibres of coarse cord or light rope, sisal or hemp, sewn into a disk and trimmed to shape. The disk should be quite thick, so it bunches, and is simply tacked in place. Coarse cord (I used a handmade Mexican 3-strand cord) for the ties, and to hold the jaws together, seems correct and looks good. (If you hang the mask, tack the support cords in place near the top, or the mask may hang out at the top.)

Before these finishing steps, you may want to round the mask at top and bottom in back; it fits the face of the wearer better that way and looks less rigid when hung. Also, pressure on the back lower edge of the chin forces the mouth closed. You will also want to clean up the inside of the mask and thin it down so it fits your face comfortably. I finished simply with oil and wax, but the proper Noh mask has a wax-like surface produced by filler and several coats of a thick paint-like enamel. Color is slightly off-white all over, with a faint tinge of red around the lips.

# CHAPTER XIV
# A Self-Portrait

## The ultimate challenge is a likeness of one's self

PORTRAITS ARE PROBABLY THE MOST EXACTING TASK for a carver, particularly self-portraits, because we don't see ourselves as "ithers see us," to quote Robert Burns. The expression we get, even if taken from a photograph, may not be the one that our friends see most often, and our view of ourselves is always a mirror image, hence reversed.

The self-portrait pictured here (Fig. 150) is particularly interesting to me because it is the first attempt at a likeness of a person by the carver, Hugh C. Minton, Jr., of Aiken, South Carolina. It is in buckeye (somewhat like basswood in reaction to tools) and is a miniature, the blank being only 3 × 3 × 5 in (7.5 × 7.5 × 12.5 cm). Height of the head from chin to top is only 3 in (7.5 cm). It was done with only knives and palm tools. No sandpaper was used before finishing with Deft®. The self-portrait was made from same-size photographic prints as a pattern, as shown (Figs. 147–149), and no templates or preliminary clay modelling were used. It is a better likeness than the photographs suggest.

In achieving such a likeness, the first step is to get the general silhouette, working from the side and front views. Then the head is rounded and modelling is begun by shaping around the nose, then the mouth and eyes. A great deal of attention must be paid to the exact shape of the nose and how it joins the rest of the face. Mr. Minton got the bridge of the nose a bit too thin and the angle between cheek and nose is too acute. Also, the nostrils are a bit small, top to bottom—all three are defects that cannot be corrected. His modelling around the mouth and chin is very good, and the slight conventionalizing of the ears is also good. I would have softened the eyelids and bulges below the eyes with wrinkle lines and drilled shallow holes to suggest pupil and iris.

When the face form is generally correct, the lining and texturing can be done. Note that Mr. Minton has achieved a facial texture that is smooth, yet still shows tool lines, a very suitable treatment. The wrinkles from the nostrils are also well handled, but the crow's-feet near the eyes are too wide, hence too prominent. This is most important, because overemphasized wrinkles convert a portrait into a caricature if one isn't careful. In addition, many carvers make the mistake of cutting away the eyebrows and the usual

*Figs. 147–149. Three photos of the subject—dead front and both sides—enlarged to size of planned carving provide precise guidance. Note hairline, crow's-feet at eye corners, Adam's apple, deep lines at sides of nose and mouth and deep-sunken eyes—all distinctive featural elements.*

bulge beneath them. Mr. Minton has handled them and the center of the brow very well, not lacing the forehead with worry lines as so many carvers do. The hairline is suggested but not emphasized; I would have softened it still more by texturing along the edges. I would also have textured the eyebrows slightly, so the treatment of moustache, eyebrows and hair would be similar.

The flow of the neck into the base is quite smooth, and the base itself is relieved in front, then chamfered geometrically, thus contrasting with the rounded contours of the head.

For a full-figure self-portrait by the author, plus additional suggestions, see *Carving Faces and Figures in Wood* in this series (cover and pages 123-127). I used templates and roughed the silhouettes with a coping saw. Mr. Minton did not; he sculptured from the block with only the tools. In the latter case, it is important to check dimensions frequently with a scale or calipers, and to stand off and look the head over from all angles regularly as you progress.

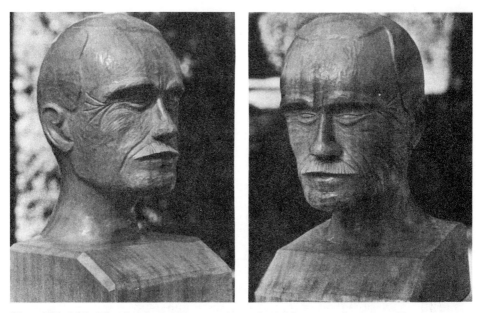

*Figs. 150–151. The finished self-portrait, undeniably a wood carving. Eye treatment would be enhanced by delineating pupils and iris and softening the upper-lid line, but facial contours in general capture the subject's personality and make the bust easily recognizable.*

# CHAPTER XV
# A Psychological Freud

AT VARIOUS TIMES AND IN VARIOUS CULTURES, artists have enjoyed depicting something in symbols, and have incorporated the symbols in such a way that they are not immediately visible. Thus there is a famous sketch of a woman seated before her mirror, which when viewed for a time becomes a head of the Devil. I have heard of a sculpture which is a face from one aspect, a lizard when turned 90°, and a turtle when turned over. I have a few pieces of red pipestone carved by Cherokee Indians which have one low-relief element blending with another, like a turtle that is also the mouth of a grotesque face, or one eye serving two faces. As a child, I made a series of sketches involving 90° rotation, so the head of an elephant became a swan, or a tub became a standing lamp, which in turn became a girl washing her feet, and so on.

This low-relief profile of Freud is possibly an outgrowth of all that, and is similar to a profile of Napoleon I carved some years ago in which the features were distinguishable in a pattern of writhing nudes. This study of Freud (Fig. 153) was an open commission for a psychology professor. It consists of a portrait in which all the lines are actually smaller low-relief carvings that become visible as you study the whole. It is in Oregon pine, 2 × 11 × 19 in (5 × 27.5 × 48 cm) carved 1 in (2.5 cm) deep. I started by making a point-to-point, life-size sketch from a photograph, then pencilled in elements that had to do with Freud's life or work as they occurred to me. Eventually, all the lines of the face were also something else, except for a few vertical lines in his goatee and moustache.

Obviously, some of the symbols and elements must be adapted to fit the immediate need, by stylizing, caricaturing, even distorting to suit. Thus the "Big C" is not upright, but turned 90°; the fallen cross requires strengthening of the line of the spirit's thigh; Gluttony and Wrath are line sketches to aid the hairy texture of the area, and so on. If a definite series, such as the Seven Deadly Sins, must all be included, you may have to strain a bit—as I did with Sloth. But the result can be a quite unique portrait.

The likeness of Freud is taken from a photograph made in the early thirties, when he was about 75 and had already broken with many of his disciples. He felt that others were stealing credit due him, and he was having increasing trouble with a debilitating illness. My effort here was to identify

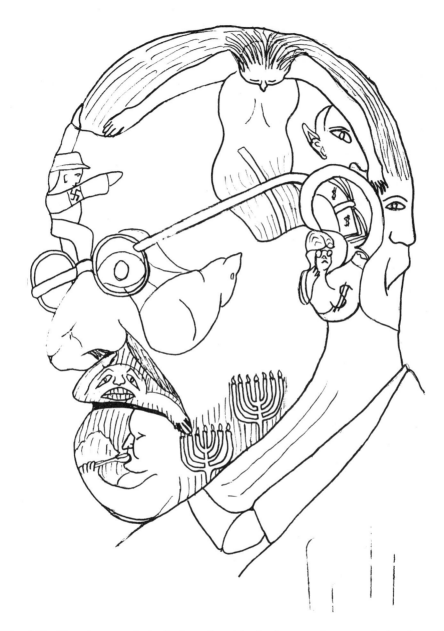

*Fig. 152. Freud, a psychological study with the face made up entirely of symbols. Wood is Oregon pine, 2 × 11 × 19 in (5 × 28 × 48 cm), carved 1 in (2.5 cm) deep around the head.*

some of his personal problems as well as to suggest the psychological problems he unmasked in all of us.

Thus, his guiding and protective spirit, the genie of his genius, is depicted as a female hovering over his brain, her hair making his. Outside her scope, however, are the increasing problems that would result in his death. First is the cancer of the mouth, detected in 1923, which ultimately killed him in 1939, shown as the "Big C" at the top of his earlobe. The other problem was the Anschlüss, the rise of Nazi influence and takeover of Austria, which ultimately drove him to England, although at this time he still felt that as a "humble scientist" he would somehow be spared or overlooked. Hence, I added the Nazi Brownshirt riding the motorcycle formed by Freud's eyeglasses.

Freud vehemently protested (in the letter from which this signature, in old German script, was copied): "Although a good Jew who has never denied his Judaism, I nevertheless cannot overlook the fact that my absolutely negative attitude to every religion, including the Jewish, separates me from the majority of our fellow Jews. . . ." However, by this time his experiences, particularly the break with Jung, a Swiss Christian, had made him trust only Jews and derogate Christians. This is depicted by the overturned cross in the bow of his glasses, and his pro-Jewishness is epitomized by the doubled Menorah of his beard.

Most of the rest of the features are the Seven Deadly Sins from Dante's *Inferno*, which Freud did much to expose in all of us. Avarice is the money bag and sheaf of bills in the ear (shown in dollars rather than marks or shillings). Next to the money and also part of the ear is Pride, a dowager with a lorgnette. At the other side of the ear (back of the head) is Jealousy or Envy. (The head of Satan above the ear is just to show that evil can sometimes prosper under the protection of a "good angel.") Lust is depicted in the nose, a rear view of a female nude with an over-developed bust; her head is Freud's eye, one arm the lines of his face, the other the bridge and right bow of his glasses. Sloth, hard to depict in anything less than a scene, is suggested by a sloth pendant from the left bow of his glasses and including the hollow of his cheek. Wrath is depicted in his moustache, Gluttony in his chin whiskers. That completes the formal portrait, about 13 motifs.

Two additional ones are happenstance. Look at his collar and tie and you have two familiar sex symbols, one of the dominant male, the other of the impotence that Freud claimed in his later years.

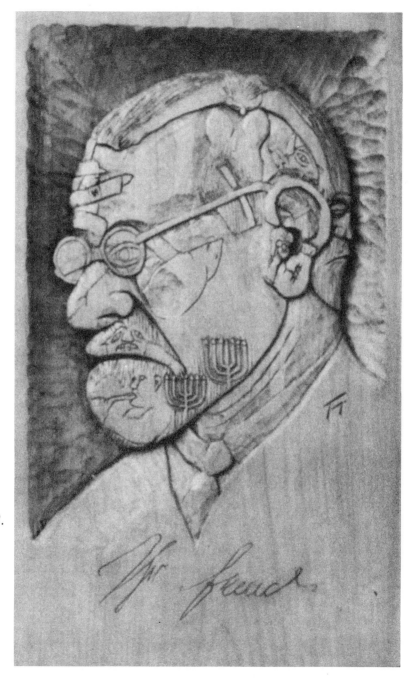

*Fig. 153.*

# CHAPTER XVI

# Swords into Plowshares

## A statuette copied from photos of an original bronze

"THEY SHALL BEAT THEIR SWORDS INTO PLOWSHARES, and their spears into pruning hooks; nation shall not lift up sword against nation, neither shall they learn war anymore." This hopeful quotation from Isaiah II:4 is quite familiar to all of us, but it is a bit ironic that the statue which symbolizes it should have been presented to the United Nations by the USSR. The 1959 original, by Evgenyi Vuchetich, bears quotation and dedication in English, moreover. It is in bronze, about 10 ft (3 m) high, and stands on a 4-ft (1.2-m) granite base.

Someone sent a postcard of the statue to a Floridian, who was so taken by it that he commissioned a copy. The work interested me because of the excellent musculature and dynamic pose, and because duplication of such a symbolic figure would be a real challenge. I decided upon walnut for the figure and the best piece available was only 2⅞ in (7 cm) thick, so about 1:12 scale was possible with a bit of planning.

All I had available was the standard color postcard, so the first step was to go to the United Nations garden to see and photograph the original. I took pictures squarely from all four sides, using the same focus and camera position so the prints would be comparable. However, even the best lens creates some distortion, particularly if the photographer is well below the center of the subject, so it was necessary to make some adjustments. A friend volunteered to undertake the onerous chore of making enlargements from the negatives so that all four views would be the same height. Scale was determined by the thickness of the walnut, but it was possible to increase size somewhat by utilizing the base wood for the body and adding a block to provide wood for the projecting left elbow. (This was a piece 1 in (2.5 cm) thick and taken from the scrap above the head.) It also seemed better to make the hammer separately and insert it, thus providing greater strength in the handle.

*Fig. 154. The original statue outside the United Nations.*

*Fig. 155. The statuette at right is 4 × 7 × 10½ in (10 × 18 × 27 cm) in walnut, over a rosewood base, and was executed from photographs of all four sides enlarged to carving size and converted to patterns. Photos provided a major guide to musculature.*

Despite the pictures and examination of the original, I found that some details, particularly in shadowed areas and around the anvil, were not clear. The anvil itself was of an unfamiliar shape, and the plowshares lying beside it were of different sizes and shapes, as well as one right- and one left-handed. Some of these dilemmas could be resolved in the sketches; the rest would have to be handled when the time came, using the overall silhouettes of the figure as a guide.

As it happened, the available walnut was longer than necessary, and the base extension proved a boon for clamping the piece during rough-cutting. The design was traced on the front and on *both* sides, taking considerable care to assure alignment. Lacking a band saw with the necessary span, and a bit worried anyhow because of the delicacy of some sections, I elected to rough out the shape from the top, using standard saws to cut away blocks, then a coping saw to silhouette sections (Fig. 156), starting with the upraised arm. The head and shoulder areas were also sawed clear and shaping begun on them to provide scale for the rest. As soon as the right fist was roughly outlined, it was drilled for the hammer handle, and the hammer itself was whittled from a scrap so the hole could be filed oval to suit the handle. Then the fist and wrist were carved more in detail.

When such a figure is carved, all views must be checked constantly and roughing must be done progressively as the carving proceeds. The head, for example, is bent forward, so it has a long neck in back and none in front, and the face is difficult to reach because of the chest and the position of the left arm. Also, the head is slightly tilted, so the ears are not level, the left being slightly higher. The same goes for the eyebrows, so this is ticklish work. It is very important to get waste wood out of the way as you go, taking off back and unimportant areas first and replacing essential lines as they are cut away.

Templates made from the sketch can be a great help in working around the head, both the outside ones, as usual, as well as the inner ones—which are more properly flat patterns. I also found a side template of help in carving the extended leg later, so that I could get the subtle locations of kneecap and muscle bulges on a twisted leg.

This is a complex action pose that is sculptural. The torso is twisted, the right arm and fist are turned, the left arm is bunched and stressed, the left leg is straight back while the right is bent; there is no relationship to the usual stiff whittled figure that has the good grace to be standing erect as if posing for a photograph. But that is the charm and vitality of the figure;

it is alive and caught off guard. What's more, the explanation of the sword-into-plowshares idea is made abundantly plain by having two finished plow-shares almost in the worker's way, while the sword itself still retains more than its normal length, thus giving emphasis to what's going on at the anvil, which is itself of an unusual shape and in an unusual position: it is sloped into the base. To emphasize this, the base for the figure itself is sloped upward from the back.

Because the wood was walnut, a number of chisels were used for the heavy carving, while the knife was limited to precise details. Included in the tools were ⅛- and ¼-in (3.2- and 6.3-mm) firmers, ¼-in (6.3-mm) gouges of varying sweeps, a veiner, V-tool, and even a 2-in (5-cm) flat gouge for smoothing areas. To do such a figure with the knife alone would take an additional week.

It should be emphasized that it is essential to rough out well ahead of the final shaping and to compare the work constantly with the sketch and several photos, so that wood is left for such bulges as the bottom of the rib cage, the forward thrust of the left shoulder, and the sex organ (if you put it in—the original, made in 1959, has a modest drape over that area).

The sword also can be a problem. It must make a graceful half-turn from hilt to point, be diamond-shaped in cross-section at the top and flattened where it lies on the anvil, and the hilt must be at a suitable angle. (I found it necessary to glue a small piece to the outer end of the hilt to make it wide enough.) To provide a front pattern, as well as a support for the vulnerable sword during roughing, I cut the front away step by step (as can be seen in Figs. 157–165), rather than cutting it out of the way initially. It provided reference points for other locations. Also, the arrangement of the anvil and plowshares is somewhat complex, so leaving extra wood there gave me some flexibility in the ultimate solution of the shape in that area. The original figure is not standing on a level base; it rises slightly from back to front. I aligned the figure itself with the grain of the wood and simply cut the bottom of the base at an angle to get the base slope.

Figures 156 to 168 show the steps clearly. Initial cuts were made with carpenter's saws, with the coping or scroll saw used after a section, such as the arm or head, was reduced in thickness. A ½-in (12.7-mm) flat gouge with a rounded end was used for much of the roughing which the saws could not reach conveniently. Areas between legs and between body and sword were multiple-drilled with about a ³⁄₁₆-in (5-mm) drill bit, then cut out with the chisel, the holes being drilled from the important side because of the possibility that they might not run straight, particularly with a portable power drill. This means that holes near the left leg were drilled through from that side, while those near the right leg were drilled from the right side. This also avoided any risk of wood breakouts. The blocks that make up the left elbow and the tip of the sword-hilt were not added until needed, and then at the end of a day's work so they wouldn't be disturbed until the glue had firmly set. (I find it almost impossible to avoid fiddling with a newly glued area, and have learned that most other people have the same problem.)

Lines indicating musculature were sketched on the figure, using various views and an anatomy text, then major ones were roughed with a ⅛-in (3.2-mm) fluter and minor ones with a veiner. The edges were faired and shaped with a small firmer or a knife, depending upon which seemed best in the particular area. The hair is a series of interrupted veiner lines, curved to indicate some curl.

This figure requires particular care in the placement and detailing of the feet. Neither has simply five toes in relaxed position. The left foot in particular is twisted around toward the left side, with the big toe spread to the right and separated from the other four. The middle three toes are in firm contact with the ground, but the little toe is almost off it and curled under because that part of the ball of the foot is lifted. Also, of course, the foot is at a compound angle with the ground. The right foot is somewhat simpler, but it is also set so that the heel is outside of center, and the big toe, longer and stronger than the others, has a firm grip on the edge of the base. Here again, the big toe is slightly separated from the others. Incidentally, this foot should not be carved until the plowshares and anvil are at least roughed in, because waste wood in the way makes carving of the toes unnecessarily difficult.

Once the elements are complete, there remains only the task of going over the figure and smoothing out rough spots or areas which create too much shadow—as some of the muscle lines may do. The base of the original was left smooth on top; I preferred to scallop mine superficially with a flat gouge. Also, the figure was finished with several coats of matte varnish to obtain a slight gloss; this suggests the sweat that a man doing such work would generate. For a sub-base, I used a block of rosewood, unfinished except for sanding and waxing. The figure itself was not touched with sandpaper, so that the tiny planes left by the tools pick up light and accentuate its strength.

*Fig. 156 (left). The walnut block proved long enough to provide an excellent clamping base, so figure was sawed out in silhouette. Close shaping of upraised arm was done with a coping saw after block thickness was halved with a cross-cut saw.*

*Fig. 157 (below). Both sides of block were laid out in careful alignment and lines replaced in each cut area. Sword was not fully outlined, to avoid losing frontal view until necessary, and head and right arm were roughed at once.*

*Fig. 158 (left). Head and shoulder templates were cut from stiff cardboard to guide shaping. Use them for frequent checks to prevent over-cutting during waste removal, since body is not in a relaxed position.*

*Fig. 159 (left). The smith's hammer, a separate piece, was made early so it could be fitted into the hand during forming. It also maintained proportions during roughing, done with larger chisels. Area before belly has been drilled.*

*Fig. 160. Because block was rather thick for coping, areas to be cut out were multiple-drilled as shown below and then cut to shape with chisels. Left elbow block and addition to sword hilt have not yet been added.*

*Fig. 161 (left). Blocks to widen left elbow and sword hilt have been glued in place and partially shaped. Holing through in front of belly and between legs is largely completed; further detailing of head and upraised arm has also been done.*

**113**

*Fig. 162 (left). Upper torso is shaped and face delineated, as well as principal outlines of head, hair and ears. Legs are being separated and outline of sword curve developed. All this work is done with block held in a woodworking vise.*

*Fig. 163 (below). More of the front waste has been removed, giving the rough outline of the sword haft and hilt, so left hand can now be shaped. Also, musculature of upper torso is being defined.*

*Fig. 164 (left). Muscle lines of neck and back are developed simultaneously with those of chest. Legs are left blocky for strength and support during this period. Head detailing progresses during rest periods in heavier cutting.*

Fig. 165 (left). Legs and sword are now completely shaped and details of plowshare positions being worked out. Head and upper torso are nearly completed.

Fig. 166 (below). Foot poses are strained in this figure and require special attention. Note cardboard leg template lying on the base. Also note difference in elevation and shape of the two buttocks.

Fig. 167 (left). Sword curve is compound and the cross-section changes from diamond-shaped to flat while a smooth curve from hilt to tip is maintained. Note details of chest and belly musculature and kneecap shape, particularly evident in this view.

*Fig. 168 (left). End of sword must appear to be beaten flat and have a plowshare shape, to lead naturally into the separate plowshares below it. Also the toes must grip the end of the base, so carving must be carefully done here.*

*Figs. 169–170. Completed figure was sawed from the base wood at a slight angle to correspond with the original, then mounted on a rosewood base of about the same proportions as the original stone pillar. Carved base is not as high proportionally, however, because the statuette will be displayed on a shelf. Note the two completed plowshares, one on each side of the special anvil that flows into the base.*

# Sharpening Can Be Done by Hand or Machine

When you buy a knife or carving chisels, they will usually be sharpened —after a fashion. The edge will have been ground and possibly whetted and honed or buffed. But the tool will require honing and stropping, particularly if you are going to use it on softer woods. If it isn't razor-sharp, it will tend to tear the surface rather than cut it.

The basic step is to form the edge by grinding, something which you should never do unless you've nicked or broken the edge, or sharpened the tool so often that the edge angle is too blunt. The problem is that grinding on modern high-speed grinders is very likely to burn the edge, and you'll have a soft tool that won't stay sharp. If you must grind, cool the tip in water twice as often as you consider necessary.

Whetting and honing are also grinding operations, but with much finer grits, and are best done by hand. Whetting is simply to rub the tool edge on a yellowish or grayish stone called *Washita*, or on the manufactured equivalent. Honing is done on a white, very hard and uniform stone called *Arkansas*, which is also the material for slips, the small shaped stones that will take the tiny burr off the inside of a gouge or V-tool. Again, you can now get a manufactured equivalent, as well as "stones" made by impregnating plastic or artificial rubber with grit.

Stropping is the final sharpening and is done on leather, first coarse with oil and an abrasive, finally on the smooth surface with oil alone. That's what a barber used to do on his straight razors; it aligns the tiny teeth of the feather edge to make the tool ultra-sharp. Remember that the barber stropped his razor each time he used it; you'll be smart to follow his example, because the edge loses alignment while not in use.

Essentially, in all the operations on a stone, the edge of the tool is moved *toward* the stone, as you would in cutting; in stropping it is *drawn away*, in the opposite direction. There are dozens of tricks in sharpening that you can learn from a good carpenter or cabinetmaker and that would be too wasteful of space to detail here.

Many woodcarvers in recent years have gone to mechanical sharpening. The simplest is to buff the tool with rouge or tripoli wax instead of honing and stropping. A simple motor setup will do it—and fits all shapes. H. M. (Mack) Sutter, Portland, Oregon, has developed relatively inexpensive and simple units for making and resharpening tools. The first and primary machine is a belt grinder which takes a 1 × 42-in (2.5 × 106-cm) belt and is available from a number of companies, including Sears, Ward and others. To this machine, Mack adds one of a series of backing blocks just above the table, the blocks conforming to the sweep of the particular tool being ground. For rough grinding, he uses a 60-grit belt. He finish-shapes with a 150-grit, and does final sharpening with a 320-grit or crocus cloth. A little care with such a setup will produce a better, straighter edge than most people can obtain on hand stones.

Next, he produces a micro-bevel on the inside or concave surface of the tool. This is minimal in width and is done with a hand stone called a *slip*, and is finished with a leather or plastic wheel and tin oxide. These wheels are mounted on a ball-bearing mandrel mounted vertically and operated at 250 to 300 rpm. He has an assortment of leather and plastic wheels 6 in (15 cm) in diameter, with edges cut to various curvatures and vees. Some of the plastic wheels are very thin, so they must be supported by thin plywood disks toward the center. Leather wheels are made of old belting glued together and shaped with harness tools. (Incidentally, a thin plastic wheel is the best device for honing the inside of very small veiners.)

Wheels of either type are coated with a thin mixture of tin oxide in kerosene. One alternative is to mix the tin-oxide powder with water to which a few drops of detergent have been added. Another is to use the very fine abrasive used in polishing eyeglasses. Both sides of each tool should be polished to a mirror finish. The final operation is to further polish with a cloth buffing wheel and tripoli wax. In the normal carving of soft woods, buffing with tripoli wax will usually handle resharpening. Also, a fine-grit 6-in (15-cm) wheel on the slow-speed mandrel will grind straight edges on firmers and V-tools without danger of burning.

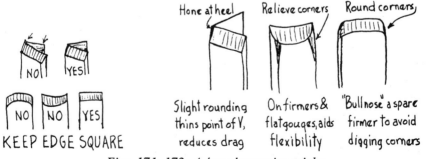

Hone at heel    Relieve corners    Round corners

NO    YES

NO    NO    YES
KEEP EDGE SQUARE

Slight rounding
thins point of V,
reduces drag

On firmers &
flat gouges, aids
flexibility

"Bullnose" a spare
firmer to avoid
digging corners

*Figs. 171–172. A few sharpening tricks.*

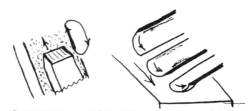

INNER BEVEL on GOUGE
After whetting, hone a very slight bevel on inner face to avoid digging in & to lengthen edge life.

STONING A FIRMER – & A GOUGE
Push edge-first (Pull on strop)   Roll & pull along

*Fig. 172.*

*Fig. 173. Mack Sutter adapted a belt sander to include a short arbor that will take a buffing wheel, as shown above. It is, in effect, an extension of the lower, driving pulley.*

**119**

Figs. 174–175. Leather and plastic wheels above are homemade and used on an arbor made by connecting an old washing-machine motor to a pulley-driven shaft, as shown below. The discs are shaped to fit the interiors of various tools.

## APPENDIX II

# The Question of Size

### How to enlarge or reduce a design to fit

IN THESE MODERN DAYS OF PURCHASED WOOD, a primary factor in carving is the kind and size of wood available. It may be sensible to design the piece to fit the wood, rather than to seek out or assemble a suitable blank. If you use commercial wood, the thickness is often a controlling factor. It may be easy to get the necessary profile dimensions, but the associated thickness may necessitate the gluing of several 1- or 2-in (2.5- or 5-cm) pieces (nowadays usually ¾ or 1½ in [1.9 or 3.8 cm] as planed) to get the needed third dimension.

Another factor in selecting size is to consider whether you plan to use tools or just a knife. Whittling is most comfortable with hand-sized pieces, of course, while woodcarving is easier on larger ones, even heroic sizes, because the work need not be anchored so securely if it is large.

I must mention other factors in selecting size: What is to be done with the piece when completed? Is it destined for a particular location, or is it going to take up more house room and be in the way if large? What sizes of tools have you? How steady is your hand and how good your eye?

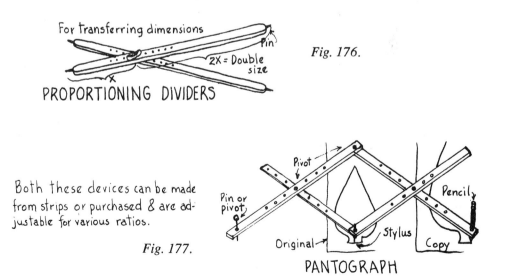

For transferring dimensions

Pin

2X = Double size

PROPORTIONING DIVIDERS

*Fig. 176.*

Both these devices can be made from strips or purchased & are adjustable for various ratios.

*Fig. 177.*

Pivot

Pin or pivot

Pencil

Original

Stylus

Copy

PANTOGRAPH

**121**

The best method of getting a correct pattern for a likeness is to get photo-graphs printed or photostats to the correct size, or to project a negative or other transparency so it can be outlined to size, either on the wood or on paper. These methods are shown in several instances in preceding chapters. But in some instances, the necessary negatives are not available and some other method must be used, or the design must be totally redrawn. Freehand redrawing is simple enough with geometric and architectural objects, but difficult with animate ones, particularly if they are complex. And for like-nesses, accuracy is important.

For a rough approximation of blank shape, the simplest method is to use a pantograph (Fig. 177) or the rather crude rubber-band method. Panto-graphs are now commercially available, but are difficult to use except from flat surface to flat surface, and they are of course limited in capacity. They can be used to reduce size by interchanging stylus and pencil. The rubber-band method is cheaper and simpler, but less accurate. The rubber band is pinned at one side of the base print, and has a pencil in the loop at the other end. An ink mark is put on the band, at the center for double size, at one-third its length from the pin for triple size, and so on. A sheet of paper, or the board itself, is placed beyond the base print, so the pencil can trace an outline while the ink mark follows the outline on the base print (Fig. 180—this is easier to do than to describe).

Many carvers use the method of squares (Fig. 178) because it is more accurate. You begin by drawing a grid over the original—or better, drawing a grid on transparent plastic or paper (so it can be re-used) and anchoring that over the print. The size of the grid is determined by the enlargement and the desired accuracy. For double size, a ⅛-in (3.2-mm) grid will do fine. Then, a corresponding ¼-in (6.3-mm) grid is drawn on the workpiece or adjacent paper for double size (or ⅜-in [9.6-mm] squares for triple size) and the design is copied square by square. (I have trouble with this method because I constantly lose my place.)

The method I use most commonly is the point-to-point (Fig. 179). To pre-pare for this, you draw a side line and a base line on the original copy, or place an L-shaped piece of cardboard or plastic in position on it, if you want to avoid damaging it. A similar side and base line is drawn on the copy paper or workpiece. Now, important dimensions are transferred one at a time. You measure at Point A in from the side and up from the base line, then multiply these dimensions by the enlargement ratio and locate the point on the copy. Thus, if Point A is 1 in (2.5 cm) in from the side

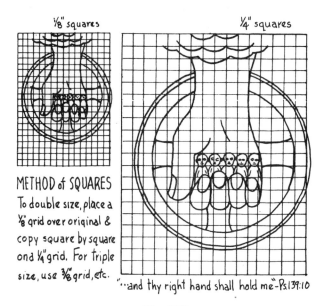

## METHOD of SQUARES

To double size, place a
⅛" grid over original &
copy square by square
on a ¼" grid. For triple
size, use ⅜" grid, etc.

"...and thy right hand shall hold me"-Ps.139:10

*Fig. 178.*

*Fig. 179.*

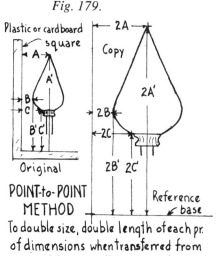

Plastic or cardboard
square

2A
Copy
A
A'
2A'
B
C
2B
B'C'
2C
Original
2B' 2C'

## POINT-to-POINT METHOD

Reference
base

To double size, double length of each pr.
of dimensions when transferred from
original to copy, all measured from
reference side & bottom lines. Connect
located points & fair-in lines.

*Fig. 180.*

Baseboard

Pin

Original

Rubber band
ink mark ⅓ of
pin-pencil distance
for triple size.
Copy

## RUBBER-BAND ENLARGING

Approximate locations & blank sizes
can be obtained this way. Shown is **3X.**

**123**

and 4 in (10 cm) up from the bottom, it would be copied 2 in (5 cm) in from the side and 8 in (20 cm) up from the bottom for double size. As many points as you consider necessary are located in this fashion. Then you join them with lines of suitable shape and fair them in. Accuracy depends upon the number of points you select, and whether or not they are clearly defined on the model. Either the method of squares or the point-to-point method can be reversed for reducing scale.

If the original is three-dimensional and there is no time to take photos, you must use a device such as proportioning dividers or calipers in transferring dimensions. (They can, by the way, also be used in the point-to-point method to avoid the computation if the enlargement is some odd ratio.)

# Make Carver's Screws

THROUGH ALL MY YEARS OF WOODCARVING, I have never used a carver's screw; clamps or a wood vise have always served my purposes. Besides, carver's screws are not stocked by some suppliers and are now very expensive, at least for this one-time machinist. However, my boyhood friend, John Phillip, now of Whittier, California, presented me with several screws of his own design recently. They are simple, inexpensive, easy to use and even to make, because the components are available in hardware stores.

To begin with, threaded stock is available, usually in 2-ft (61-cm) lengths, from stores such as Sears. They also sell lag screws of various sizes. If you have the tools available, you can drill and tap the end of a piece of threaded stock to take a ¼- or ⁵⁄₁₆-in (6.3- or 8-mm) lag screw with the head cut off and the shank threaded. Even simpler is to get a long lag screw of the desired diameter, cut off the head and thread the shank. Either of these designs can be equipped with spacers cut from pipe (⅜- or ½-in [9.6- or 12.7-mm] diameter) washers and double nuts. The double nuts are necessary to screw the screw into the wood blank, but after that only a single one is needed. Beyond that, all you need do is to drill a hole of suitable diameter in your bench or other work table, and you're ready to go.

It is even simpler, in the absence of threading tools, to buy a lag screw of suitable length (about 4 in [10 cm] for the usual 2-in [5-cm]-thick bench top), and simply use it directly as a carver's screw. If it is too long, washers can be added beneath the bench top.

An adjustable open-end wrench tightens and loosens either lag screw or single nut on the designs first mentioned. It is possible, of course, to be more elaborate and to make a wing nut like those commonly supplied with a carver's screw, or you may find a conventional wing nut with suitable thread. An alternative is to drill two opposed flats of a hexagonal nut and drive in short pins to make a wing nut of sorts, but I find it more secure to tighten the screw with a wrench so it will withstand fairly strong blows at the upper end of a blank.

The depth a carver's screw is driven into the blank depends upon the height of the blank and the amount of force you expect to exert at the top. Too short a screw will pull, especially in soft woods like pine or bass. Too long a screw may project through the base on small carvings. (As a matter

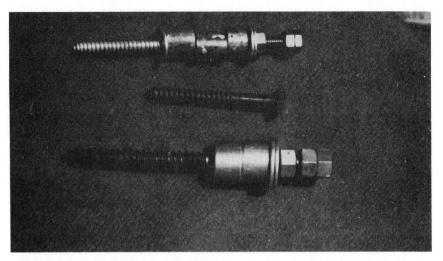

*Fig. 181. Small carver's screws can be made from lag bolts either by cutting off the head and rethreading the shank for standard hex nuts (top and bottom) or by using the lag screw without change. Pipe spacers (top) should be flanked by washers to increase bearing surface.*

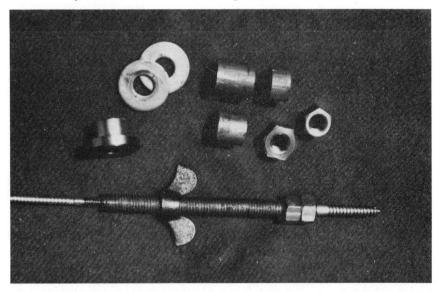

*Fig. 182. Threaded stock, in this case ½-in (12.7-mm), can be drilled and tapped for ¼-in- (6.3-mm-)diameter lag screws with heads cut off and shanks threaded. It may also be possible to get wing nuts to fit. The screw shown was cut in half to make two.*

of fact, I have seen small German carvings with integral bases—say, of a deer or a dog in woodland—in which a stump is carved beneath the animal's body. It is there to cover what would otherwise be a hole from the carver's screw.) Also, the carver's screw should be inserted in a drilled pilot hole to reduce the danger of splitting, and the screw itself should be large enough to avoid being bent when it is driven in or under stress of carving. I have found that by drilling the hole for the screw near the outer corner of the bench enables me to work around the piece well enough so that frequent adjustments of the screw are not required. A short carver's screw can also be used to hold a panel for relief carving.

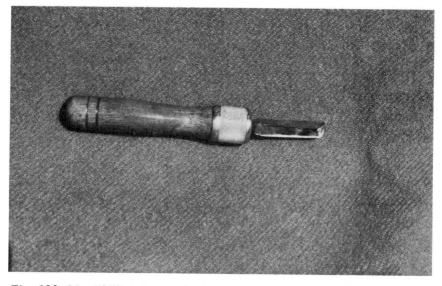

*Fig. 183. Mr. Phillip also made this knife from a cut-off high-speed-steel lathe tool bit. It is unusual in that it is sharpened on both sides and on the end, so it can be used as a chisel. It is similar to a tool the Chinese make for carving ivory.*

# Index